Oriens

ORIENS

A Pilgrimage Through Advent and Christmas

November 28, 2021 – February 2, 2022

FR. JOEL SEMBER

Our Sunday Visitor
Huntington, Indiana

Nihil Obstat
Msgr. Michael Heintz, Ph.D.
Censor Librorum

Imprimatur
✠ Kevin C. Rhoades
Bishop of Fort Wayne-South Bend
June 8, 2021

The *Nihil Obstat* and *Imprimatur* are official declarations that a book is free from doctrinal or moral error. It is not implied that those who have granted the *Nihil Obstat* and *Imprimatur* agree with the contents, opinions, or statements expressed.

Except where noted, the Scripture citations used in this work are taken from the New American Bible, revised edition © 2010, 1991, 1986, 1970 Confraternity of Christian Doctrine, Washington, DC, and are used by permission of the copyright owner. All rights reserved. No part of the New American Bible may be reproduced in any form without permission in writing from the copyright owner.

Excerpts from the English translation of The Roman Missal © 2010, International Commission on English in the Liturgy Corporation (ICEL); All rights reserved.

Excerpts from the Book of Blessings, © 1988, Confraternity of Christian Doctrine, Inc., Washington, DC. Used with permission. All rights reserved. No portion of this text may be reproduced by any means without permission in writing from the copyright owner. United States Conference of Catholic Bishops, Washington, DC.

Every reasonable effort has been made to determine copyright holders of excerpted materials and to secure permissions as needed. If any copyrighted materials have been inadvertently used in this work without proper credit being given in one form or another, please notify Our Sunday Visitor in writing so that future printings of this work may be corrected accordingly.

Copyright © 2021 by Father Joel Sember
26 25 24 23 22 21   1 2 3 4 5 6 7 8 9

All rights reserved. With the exception of short excerpts for critical reviews, no part of this work may be reproduced or transmitted in any form or by any means whatsoever without permission from the publisher. For more information, visit: www.osv.com/permissions.

Our Sunday Visitor Publishing Division
Our Sunday Visitor, Inc.
200 Noll Plaza
Huntington, IN 46750
1-800-348-2440

ISBN: 978-1-68192-730-5 (Inventory No. T2600)
eISBN: 978-1-68192-731-2
LCCN: 2021940494

Cover design: Melissa Schlegel
Cover art: Lisa Dorschner
Interior design: Amanda Falk

PRINTED IN THE UNITED STATES OF AMERICA

Dedicated to Saint Joseph,
foster father of Jesus
and father of spiritual fatherhood

+

and to James and Marion Sember
and family who keep me humble

+

and to all my fellow pilgrims
who walked with me on
Oriens 2020 last year

+

¡Buen Camino!

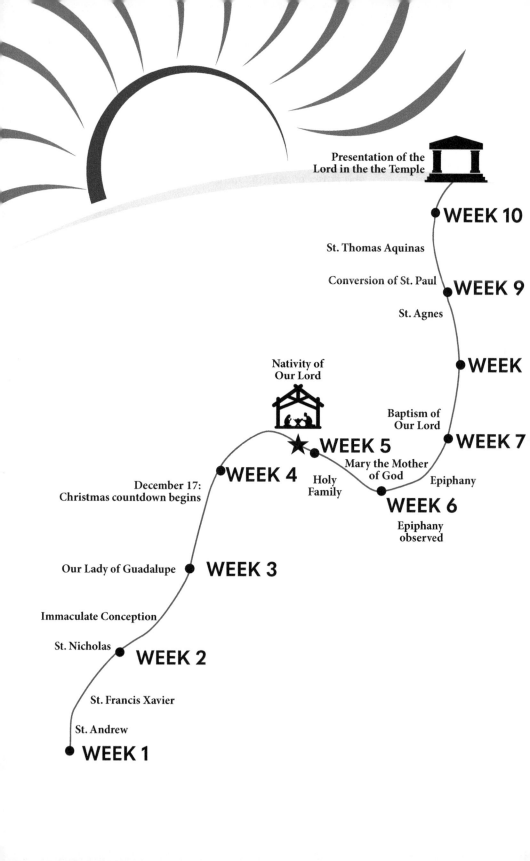

Presentation of the
Lord in the the Temple

WEEK 10

St. Thomas Aquinas

Conversion of St. Paul

WEEK 9

St. Agnes

WEEK

Nativity of
Our Lord

Baptism of
Our Lord

WEEK 7

WEEK 5

Mary the Mother
of God

WEEK 4

Holy
Family

Epiphany

December 17:
Christmas countdown begins

WEEK 6

Epiphany
observed

Our Lady of Guadalupe

WEEK 3

Immaculate Conception

St. Nicholas

WEEK 2

St. Francis Xavier

St. Andrew

WEEK 1

Contents

Introduction

Give a man a fish, you feed him for a day.
Teach a man to pray, and you feed him for a lifetime.

TEACH A MAN TO PRAY ...

There are many wonderful Advent books full of moving meditations for you to choose from. This isn't one of them. Instead of giving you meditations I came up with, *Oriens* will teach you how to meditate for yourself. If you don't really know how to pray with Scripture, this book will teach you. If you already know how to pray, then it will help you to pray better. I left space each day for you to journal your prayer experiences. When you get to the end of the book, you will find it is full of moving meditations, but they won't be my meditations; they'll be yours. I hope that, as you learn to go deeper in your conversations with God, prayer becomes your favorite part of each day, and this season takes on a whole new meaning.

"DO YOU WANT TO WALK THE CAMINO WITH ME?"

It was my third year of Theology at the North American College in Rome. We had two weeks of Easter vacation to go experience Europe. A classmate and I decided to walk the *Camino Portugués*, a shorter version of the famous medieval pilgrimage route across Spain. (It's so famous that it's called simply *El Camino*, which means "The Way" in Spanish.) I bought some shoes and borrowed a backpack, and we flew to Lisbon. We took a train to the Portuguese border and spent a week walking to the burial place of Saint James the apostle. Something special happened *on the way*. I started to see myself, and the ordinary world, in a whole new way. I discovered the magic of walking pilgrimages.

Three years later I was back in America as a newly ordained priest. "We don't have to fly to Europe to walk down the road," I thought. I scoped out a walking route to a local shrine, lined up places to stay every twelve miles or so, and found people to bring us food each night. Twenty-two people joined me on that pilgrimage. Their lives were changed, and I realized that the magic of walking pilgrimages isn't limited to the plains of Spain. Every year for the past ten years, I've led a five-day walking pilgrimage to the Shrine of Our Lady of Good Help in Champion, Wisconsin. I never cease to come away with some new gift, blessing, or lesson learned on the way.

Walking pilgrimages are a much different experience from a bus pilgrimage. When you ride a bus to a shrine, it's mostly about the destination. Pilgrims look forward to a big "Aha" moment waiting for them when they arrive. Walking pilgrims, on the other hand, learn the joy of the journey. They see familiar roads in a whole new way. They appreciate the beauty around them. They enter into the ebb and flow of nature. They draw closer to the people they walk with. They learn to keep their eyes open for encounters with God along the way. Most of all, they learn to put one foot in front of the other and keep walking no matter what. A walking pilgrimage is about more than the destination; it's a journey of the heart. It changes you in ways you never expected.

THE ADVENT JOURNEY

So, what does this have to do with Advent and Christmas? We all struggle with Advent. The Church is telling us to slow down, but the world is telling us, "Hurry up." We rush around preparing for the birth of Jesus. We look forward to the big "Aha" moment waiting for us at Christmas. And we always seem to miss out somehow. How is it that every year Christmas seems less merry and bright than we were hoping it would be? Too often, Christmas seems to fly by even more quickly than Advent does!

The problem is that we keep treating Advent like the bus on the way to Christmas. We expect to step off at Bethlehem and have some kind of amazing experience. Yet Holy Mother Church designed Advent to be more like a walking pilgrimage. You take a little step every day. You learn to enjoy the journey instead of rushing to Christmas — and then you're better prepared to enjoy the full Christmas season, rather than rushing to get the celebration over with. You connect with the people around you. You enter into a new rhythm. The ordinary things of life start to take on a new meaning. God meets you on the road. Think of this book as a Camino guidebook. It will show you how to step off the busy Christmas bus and walk the Advent road one day at a time. You will learn that Advent and Christmas are more than a destination; they involve a journey of the heart.

KEEP WALKING

This book lasts nearly ten weeks, from the first Sunday of Advent on November 28 to the feast of the Presentation on February 2. The feast of the Presentation (also called Candlemas) is the traditional final day after which Christmas decorations must be taken down. That way you will get 27 days to prepare for Christmas and forty days to celebrate Christmas (kind of like the forty days of Lent followed by the fifty days of Easter). We need those extra days. None of the people who saw the Christ Child in person understood the true meaning of Christmas. It was only in the days and years afterward that the "dawn from on high" began to rise in their hearts (see Lk 1:78). The same is true for us in our ongoing journey of faith. Praying with this devotional until February 2 will help you continue to see Jesus in the ordinary. Besides, it's easier to pray in the post-Christmas lull, and we need a little help getting through the low time in January.

You don't have to walk the whole way with me; it's your journey and you can quit any time. But let me encourage you to plan for a longer walk. Consider putting up your Christmas tree a little later this year. Put on the lights and ornaments, but don't plug in the lights until the Light of the World is born on December 25. Then keep your tree lit all through the twelve days until January 6. Plan to keep at least your Advent wreath and Nativity scene up until February 2. It may seem like a long way to go now, but you'll be surprised at how quickly it passes. And you'll really enjoy those extra days.

IF YOU MISS A DAY

Even when you are too busy to pray, try to at least open this book and read the Scripture passage each day. If you end up missing a day or two (or even a week), don't try to go back and do all the meditations you missed. Just skip ahead to the current day and pray that one well. It is not important that you do every single meditation. What matters is that you put your heart into your prayer. Prayer is experiencing how our Father looks at you with love. Holiness is learning to live in his long, loving gaze every moment of your life.

You might assume because I wrote this book that I'm great at praying. Far from it! I was trained as a spiritual director through the Institute for Priestly Formation. I have taught countless numbers of people how to pray. I've been on pilgrimages and retreats and even a thirty-day silent retreat. But the truth is, unless I'm actually on a retreat or a pilgrimage, I usually pray badly. Most days I'm too busy, distracted, self-absorbed, or lazy to really pray well. And the problem is compounded during the busy Advent and Christmas season. I wrote this book because I need it too! I will be praying with you and for you this whole season. Please pray for me and for your fellow *Oriens* pilgrims. We each make our own journey, and every journey is unique, but no one walks alone. ¡*Buen Camino!*

Fr. Joel Sember
Priest, Pastor, Pilgrim

Suggested Calendar for the Advent and Christmas Season

November 28, 1st Sunday of Advent: Light the first candle on your Advent wreath.

December 5, 2nd Sunday of Advent: Light the second candle on your Advent wreath.

December 6 (Monday): Give some treats for Saint Nicholas Day.

December 8 (Wednesday): Solemnity of the Immaculate Conception. Put up your crèche (manger scene).

December 12, 3rd Sunday of Advent: Light the third (rose) candle on your Advent wreath.

December 13 (Monday): Do some research on traditions surrounding the feast of Saint Lucy.

Before December 17: Put up your Christmas tree. Decorate it, but don't plug the lights in. Wait until the Light of the World is born.

December 19, 4th Sunday of Advent: Light the fourth candle on your Advent wreath.

December 24/25: After attending Christmas Mass, put the Baby Jesus in the crèche and light up your Christmas tree. Change the candles in your Advent wreath to white.

January 1 (Saturday): Octave Day of Christmas, solemnity of Mary, Mother of God. Start the new year with Mary.

January 6 (Thursday): Epiphany. Have a family party to bless your home with blessed chalk. Afterward you can take down the tree (if you want to) and the decorations, but don't take down the Advent wreath or the crèche.

January 22 (Saturday): A day of penance in the United States in reparation for violations to the dignity of the human person committed through acts of abortion, and prayer for the full restoration of the legal guarantee to the right to life.

February 2 (Wednesday): Feast of the Presentation. Have one last Christmas party! Light the candles on your wreath and have a family Candlemas procession to the crèche. Sing Christmas carols. Then put away any remaining Christmas decorations.

Blessing of an Advent Wreath

The use of the Advent Wreath is a traditional practice which has found its place in the Church as well as in the home. The blessing of an Advent Wreath takes place on the First Sunday of Advent or on the evening before the First Sunday of Advent. When the blessing of the Advent Wreath is celebrated in the home, it is appropriate that it be blessed by a parent or another member of the family.

All make the sign of the cross together: + In the name of the Father, and of the Son, and of the Holy Spirit.
Leader: Our help is in the name of the Lord.
Response: Who made heaven and earth.
Leader: A reading from the book of the Prophet Isaiah:

> *The people who walked in darkness*
>   *have seen a great light;*
> *Upon those who dwelt in the land of gloom*
>   *a light has shone.*
> *You have brought them abundant joy*
>   *and great rejoicing;*
> *As they rejoice before you as at the harvest,*
>   *as men make merry when dividing spoils. ...*
> *For a child is born to us, a son is given us;*
>   *upon his shoulder dominion rests.*
> *They name him Wonder-Counselor, God-Hero,*
>   *Father-Forever, Prince of Peace.*
> *His dominion is vast*
>   *and forever peaceful,*
> *From David's throne, and over his kingdom,*
>   *which he confirms and sustains.*
> *By judgment and justice,*
>   *both now and forever. (Is 9:1-2, 5-6)*

Leader: The Word of the Lord.
Response: Thanks be to God.

Leader: Let us pray.

Lord our God,
we praise you for your Son, Jesus Christ:
He is Emmanuel, the hope of the peoples;
he is the wisdom that teaches and guides us;
he is the Savior of every nation.

Lord God,
let your blessing come upon us
as we light the candles of this wreath.
May the wreath and its light
be signs of Christ's promise to bring us salvation.
May he come quickly and not delay.

We ask this through Christ our Lord.

Response: Amen.

The blessing may conclude with a verse from "O Come, O Come, Emmanuel":

O come, desire of nations, bind
in one the hearts of humankind.
Bid ev'ry sad division cease,
and be thyself our Prince of peace.
Rejoice! Rejoice! Emmanuel
shall come to thee, O Israel.

— From *Book of Blessings*

Week One

Lectio Divina

This first week we will use an ancient prayer form called *lectio divina* (pronounced LEK-si-o di-VEE-na). It has four simple steps, known by their Latin names: *lectio* (reading), *meditatio* (meditation), *oratio* (prayer), and *contemplatio* (contemplation). Don't worry about each Latin word. The prayer form is as simple as this: Read, Think, Talk, Listen.

We begin with a prayerful reading of a passage from Scripture. We turn over in our minds what we have read: What was the cultural context? What does this particular word mean? What does this mean to me? We chew on the passage for a while. Perhaps a particular word, phrase, or idea speaks to us. But it won't really be prayer if we just stay in our heads. So, we speak to God in our heart or out loud. A conversation takes two, so for the last part of *lectio*, we adopt an attitude of receiving. We are talking, then we are listening. Many people find the *contemplatio* to be a difficult step; they worry about if they are "doing it right" or "if it's really God" whose voice they hear. Don't try too hard. Just be quiet and receive for a little while. Prayer is not so much about getting something from God as it is just being with God. We are using Scripture as a conversation starter, but conversations with God go deeper than words. I'll walk you through it.

Grace of the Week: Each week has a particular theme or focus. The first week will focus on the creation from the perspective of human beings. The simplest things can be the easiest to forget, and the most profound when they are rediscovered. Pray for the grace to wonder anew at the marvel, mystery, and miracle of being God's creation.

November 28 — Sunday
First Sunday of Advent

Happy Advent! Are you ready for this journey? If so, you're already doing better than I am. I'm never quite ready for Advent to begin. Fortunately, Advent is a time of preparation. As we walk together toward Christmas, you'll find yourself slowly becoming more prepared. We must prepare our hearts and our homes for the coming of Christ.

READ TODAY'S SCRIPTURE PASSAGE:
LUKE 21:25–28, 34–36

[Jesus said to his disciples:] "There will be signs in the sun, the moon, and the stars, and on earth nations will be in dismay, perplexed by the roaring of the sea and the waves. People will die of fright in anticipation of what is coming upon the world, for the powers of the heavens will be shaken. And then they will see the Son of Man coming in a cloud with power and great glory. But when these signs begin to happen, stand erect and raise your heads because your redemption is at hand.

"Beware that your hearts do not become drowsy from carousing and drunkenness and the anxieties of daily life, and that day catch you by surprise like a trap. For that day will assault everyone who lives on the face of the earth. Be vigilant at all times and pray that you have the strength to escape the tribulations that are imminent and to stand before the Son of Man."

You have twenty-seven days until Christmas. You have to accomplish shopping, decorating, baking, party planning, card sending, Christmas special-watching, quality time with family and friends, an awkward party or two … and you don't even know what unexpected twists might await you! Now you understand what Jesus means when he says, "*People will die of fright in anticipation of what is coming upon the world.*" We get nervous just thinking about Advent, much less the end of the world! But we don't want our hearts to become drowsy from eggnog and Christmas cookies. We want our hearts to be awake to the loving presence of God.

What do you most remember from Christmas last year? Was it the gifts, the decorations, the baked goods, the parties, the cards … all the things you stress about? Or was it something else? Let your mind drift back to last year and perhaps journal whatever you remember.

Now go back and read the Scripture passage a second time.

The coming of Jesus should excite us. We should *stand erect and raise our heads* knowing that our Lord and Savior is on his way to meet us. We must be vigilant to meet the Lord — in Latin, *vigilate*. The vigils were the night watches; soldiers would stay up and watch to protect the camp from attacks that might happen under cover of darkness. (We will see these words again in Lk 2:8.) But watching for the Lord means not so much sleepless nights, but a watchful heart. A prayerful heart is a watchful heart. So, to do Advent well, we need to be prepared to pray well.

I have found that these two ingredients help me to pray well: place and time.

PLACE FOR PRAYER

Where will you pray? If you don't already have a prayer room or a prayer corner, make one. It can be a whole spare room, or as simple as a prayer chair or one side of a couch. Put distractions, like the remote and the mobile phone, out of reach. Hang some pictures or images or an inspiring Scripture quote. It should be free of distractions and full of things that help you focus on God. Some people like to light a candle while they are praying (but do not leave candles unattended). Plan a *place* for prayer.

TIME FOR PRAYER

When will you pray? I like to pray right when I get up in the morning. Some people like to pray in the quiet of the evening. It may not happen exactly as you planned every day, but if you don't plan it, chances are it won't happen. Plan a *time* for prayer.

Also plan how you will prepare for Christmas this year. Remember, Christmas is not the only stop on our journey. We will stop to enjoy Saint

Nicholas Day on December 6. Immaculate Conception is a holy day of obligation, so plan to attend Mass on Wednesday, December 8. When will you put up your Christmas tree? Try to make it a family event. Whenever you put up your Christmas tree, I encourage you not to light it until after Christmas Mass. When will you put out your Christmas crèche? Take some time to plan these activities in advance.

For now, the only thing you need to do is put out the Advent wreath and light the first candle. Everything else can happen in time. While you're looking at your calendar, you might want to plan a little time for baking, sending cards, present wrapping, and quality family time — whatever makes Christmas special for you. But let's not just plan Christmas; let's also pray through Christmas. You "stand before the Son of Man" every time you pray. Ask God for the strength to pray well this Advent season. Ask God to show you his plans for your Christmas and help you accomplish them. Ask God to help you focus on the things that really matter and to let go of the things that don't matter.

And it starts with a simple question: What do you *really want* for Christmas this year?

Consider this question, then read the Scripture passage a third time and just be open to the nudge of the Holy Spirit.

SUGGESTIONS FOR JOURNALING

Every day I will offer a few questions or thoughts to help you journal. Some people find that they already have plenty to journal about and don't need these questions. Other people find the suggestions help them pull more out of their daily prayer. I encourage you to do whatever works for you; it's your journey.

1. My favorite thing about last Christmas was …
2. I get the most joy from …
3. Last Christmas I struggled the most with …
4. What do I want to make sure to do? What do I want to make sure not to do?
5. What is God's desire for my Christmas journey?
6. Where and when will I pray?
7. I most deeply desire …

Now, just be still for a moment; the Lord is here with you.

The most important part of our Advent journey is an attitude of thanksgiving. So, thank God for today's prayer time and close with an Our Father.

November 29 — Monday
Monday of the First Week of Advent

Preparation: *Come, Holy Spirit, enlighten the eyes of my heart* (see Eph 1:18).

Lectio: Our pilgrimage begins with the creation story, but perhaps not the version you might have been expecting. The Bible tells the story of creation twice. The first story shows how creation unfolds in an orderly way over the course of six "days," starting with light and ending with the creation of man and woman (see Gn 1:1—2:4). The second story tells it from the opposite perspective, beginning with the creation of man. Read through the passage slowly and prayerfully, and try to see it with fresh eyes.

GENESIS 2:4–7
This is the story of the heavens and the earth at their creation. When the LORD God made the earth and the heavens — there was no field shrub on earth and no grass of the field had sprouted, for the LORD God had sent no rain upon the earth and there was no man to till the ground, but a stream was welling up out of the earth and watering all the surface of the ground — then the LORD God formed the man out of the dust of the ground and blew into his nostrils the breath of life, and the man became a living being.

Meditatio: The ancients understood that when a human being dies he will turn into dust. So, our ancient authors pictured God starting from dust and ending with a well-formed human being, like a potter molding clay. There is a play here on words between the Hebrew *adam* (man) and *adama* (ground). Picture the care with which God shapes the bones, muscles, eyes, teeth, and hair. Then God bends down and shares some of his own life with this being. The Hebrew word for "breath" (*ruach*) also means "spirit" and "wind." It is as though the creature lives because God has shared some of his own life with it. What would it feel like to be created? Think about what it means to be shaped by God, to bear his fingerprints on your body and his warm breath in your lungs. Then read the passage again.

Oratio: The first thing Adam would see when he woke up was the God who had just created him, perhaps beaming proudly at his new creation, like an artist admiring his masterpiece. Look at God, and let him look at you. What words come to your mind? Speak to your Creator. Ask him about yourself or about him, or just thank him for creating you. Take some deep breaths. Then read the passage one more time.

Contemplatio: Open your heart to receive whatever God might want to give you. Don't sweat this step. Think of it like sensing the direction of the wind or basking for a moment in the sun's light. Contemplation is about being, but being in relationship. Just be with the God who has created you and is proud of the work he has done. Receive his love for you in whatever way you can.

SUGGESTIONS FOR JOURNALING

1. What was my most noticeable thought, feeling, or desire during prayer time today?
2. What was on my heart? What did I bring to God?
3. Did I notice God's presence or his response to me in any particular way? If I did, how would I describe that? If not, how did I feel about that?
4. Does it feel different to look at my own hands and realize they were shaped by God, and that no one else has my fingerprints?
5. One day I will take my final breath. What does each breath mean to me? How do my breaths connect me with God? What do my breaths mean to God?

Spend a few minutes in wonder and awe at the mystery and marvel of creation that is you! Let gratitude rise in your heart. Then close with an Our Father.

November 30 — Tuesday

Tuesday of the First Week of Advent

SAINT ANDREW, APOSTLE

Andrew is less well known than his brother Simon Peter, but he was the one who introduced his brother to Jesus (see Jn 1:35–42). Andrew is said to have preached the Gospel in Greece, where he suffered martyrdom at Patras. Bound by ropes to an X-shaped cross, he preached to the crowds for two days until he was overcome by death. He is the patron of Greece, Scotland, and Russia. There is a tradition of beginning a Christmas novena on his feast day. The name Andrew actually comes from a Greek word meaning manly or masculine. What does it mean to be manly? Perhaps today's Scripture passage will enlighten us.

Preparation: *Come, Holy Spirit, enlighten the eyes of my heart.* Flip back, and briefly review yesterday's prayer time.

Lectio: Ask God to help you wonder anew at the marvel, mystery, and miracle of his creation. Read the passage below, slowly and prayerfully. Notice what jumps out to you as you read.

GENESIS 2:8–9,15–17

The Lord God planted a garden in Eden, in the east, and placed there the man whom he had formed. Out of the ground the Lord God made grow every tree that was delightful to look at and good for food, with the tree of life in the middle of the garden and the tree of the knowledge of good and evil.

The Lord God then took the man and settled him in the garden of Eden, to cultivate and care for it. The Lord God gave the man this order: You are free to eat from any of the trees of the garden except the tree of knowledge of good and evil. From that tree you shall not eat; when you eat from it you shall die.

Meditatio: The creation that surrounds man was made for him to feed him and delight him. Some theologians interpret the various trees as symbolizing all the pleasures and delights of life; he lives in a veritable "garden of delight" (one possible meaning for the word "Eden"). The world was made for him, but it does not belong to him; both he and his home belong to the God who made them. This God entrusts man with a specific job, "to cultivate and care for it." Picture the kind of fancy, cultivated gardens that often surround European mansions. God is the master and man is the gardener or caretaker. He can use everything except for one single tree that is off-limits. What thoughts or feelings arise in your heart? Read the passage again prayerfully.

Oratio: When have you experienced being a steward of God's creation? What has God entrusted to you — life, land, children to care for, gifts of talents? Have you used them in ways that made the master proud of you? Have you respected the rules he has set for his garden? God is here with you and ready to listen. Speak to him from your heart. Then read the passage one more time.

Contemplatio: Open your heart and let your master speak to you. Receive whatever it is that God wants to give you. You are his steward, his caretaker, his friend. Rest quietly for a minute or two and marvel at all that has been entrusted to you.

SUGGESTIONS FOR JOURNALING
1. What most delights me about the creation that surrounds me?
2. How do I see myself as a steward of creation? What has been entrusted to me?
3. How has God set rules or limits for me? What things are "off-limits" to me because I am the steward and not the master?
4. I feel most humbled by ...
5. I felt God saying to me ...
6. I left prayer wanting ...

After you've journaled, spend a minute in gratitude for the prayer time you've just had. Then close with the Saint Andrew Novena Prayer:

Hail and blessed be the hour and moment in which the Son of God was born of the most pure Virgin Mary, at midnight, in Bethlehem, in the piercing cold. In that hour vouchsafe, I beseech Thee, O my God, to hear my prayer and grant my desires, [here mention your request] through the merits of Our Savior Jesus Christ, and of His blessed Mother. Amen.

December 1 — Wednesday
Wednesday of the First Week of Advent

Preparation: *Come, Holy Spirit, enlighten the eyes of my heart.* Flip back to yesterday's prayer and recall a blessing you experienced. Spend a minute savoring God's loving care for all his creatures and especially his care for you.

Lectio: In your own words ask God to help you wonder anew at the marvel, mystery, and miracle of his creation. Read today's passage slowly and prayerfully.

GENESIS 2:18–25

The LORD God said: It is not good for the man to be alone. I will make a helper suited to him. So the LORD God formed out of the ground all the wild animals and all the birds of the air, and he brought them to the man to see what he would call them; whatever the man called each living creature was then its name. The man gave names to all the tame animals, all the birds of the air, and all the wild animals; but none proved to be a helper suited to the man.

So the LORD God cast a deep sleep on the man, and while he was asleep, he took out one of his ribs and closed up its place with flesh. The LORD God then built the rib that he had taken from the man into a woman. When he brought her to the man, the man said:

*"This one, at last, is bone of my bones
    and flesh of my flesh;
This one shall be called 'woman,'
    for out of man this one has been taken."*

That is why a man leaves his father and mother and clings to his wife, and the two of them become one body.

The man and his wife were both naked, yet they felt no shame.

Meditatio: God makes all kinds of living beings, and the man helps by naming each one (in the Bible, naming something is a sign of authority over it). Despite all the delights that surround him, something is missing that the man can't quite name. Only when he wakes up to the woman of his dreams does he realize his desire to have a relationship with someone who can receive his love and love him in return. Man was made by love and for love. The two are perfectly comfortable together. Read the passage again slowly.

Oratio: What is this prayer time stirring up inside of you? Is something missing in your life that you can't quite name? Notice the feelings that are stirring inside of you, then speak to God honestly about them. You can be perfectly comfortable with God. Share your heart with the one who made it. When you are done talking, read the passage one more time, or just the word or phrase that really spoke to you.

Contemplatio: Open your heart to conversation with God. The one who made you knows your deepest desires. He also knows his plans to fulfill them. What is it that God wants to give you, or might be saying back to you? Don't try too hard to "get it." Just be open to receive.

SUGGESTIONS FOR JOURNALING
1. Which of the animals God has created most delights me?
2. How have I cooperated with God's work of creation, working alongside God in my own little way?
3. Was there a time in my life when I experienced a longing that I didn't understand or couldn't really name?
4. My life seemed to click when …
5. I ended prayer wanting …

After you've journaled, close with a brief conversation giving thanks to God for your prayer experience. Then pray an Our Father.

December 2 — Thursday

Thursday of the First Week of Advent

Preparation: *Come, Holy Spirit, enlighten the eyes of my heart.* Flip back to yesterday's prayer and recall a blessing you experienced. Spend a minute savoring God's loving care for all his creatures and especially his care for you.

Lectio: In your own words ask God to help you wonder anew at the marvel, mystery, and miracle of human and divine love. Some people are scandalized to discover a love poem right in the middle of the Bible. They don't seem to realize that the Bible begins with a wedding (see Gn 2:18–25) and ends with a wedding (Rv 19:1–9). Do you think God might be trying to tell us something? Read today's passage slowly and prayerfully.

SONG OF SONGS 2:8–14

The sound of my lover! here he comes
  springing across the mountains,
  leaping across the hills.
My lover is like a gazelle
  or a young stag.
See! He is standing behind our wall,
  gazing through the windows,
  peering through the lattices.
My lover speaks and says to me,
  "Arise, my friend, my beautiful one,
  and come!
For see, the winter is past,
  the rains are over and gone.
The flowers appear on the earth,
  the time of pruning the vines has come,
  and the song of the turtledove is heard in our land.

The fig tree puts forth its figs,
    and the vines, in bloom, give forth fragrance.
"Arise, my friend, my beautiful one,
    and come!
My dove in the clefts of the rock,
    in the secret recesses of the cliff,
Let me see your face,
    let me hear your voice,
For your voice is sweet,
    and your face is lovely."

Meditatio: More than anything, two people who love each other long to be together. This poem is full of the longing between young lovers. When was the first time you fell in love? What did it feel like? How did it change you? We sometimes chuckle when our siblings, friends, or children fall deeply in love. They act like they are the first people in the world to ever be in love, and no one has ever experienced something so amazing as this! And yet, when we reflect on our own experiences, we realize that falling in love always catches us off guard and sweeps us along. Even when you fall in love again with a spouse after twenty or thirty years of marriage, it is like tasting an old wine that surprises us with how good it has gotten. There is something about true love that is always fresh and new. Notice what word or phrase really speaks to you as you read this passage a second time.

Oratio: What thoughts, feelings, or desires are rising in your heart? They may also be fears, failures, or disappointments. Love is the most beautiful, powerful, and poignant experience. And that also means it can be the most difficult, devastating, and heartbreaking experience. But you have never experienced it alone. Because God is love, every experience of real love is an experience of God. Turn to the God who loves you. Share with him what is on your heart. Be completely honest with him. When you have poured out your heart, read the passage a third time slowly and prayerfully.

Contemplatio: God knows the depths of your heart just like he knew the desires in Adam's heart. Now receive what God wants to share with you.

Is there some new insight or understanding that emerges? How does your experience look different in the light of God's love? Rest in his love for you for a few minutes before moving on.

SUGGESTIONS FOR JOURNALING

1. Falling in love is like …
2. I am afraid that …
3. God wanted me to know …
4. The deepest desire that I have right now is for …
5. I feel most satisfied, joyful, and peaceful when …
6. I ended prayer wanting …

After you've journaled, close with a conversation with God giving thanks for your prayer experience. Then pray an Our Father.

December 3 — Friday
Friday of the First Week of Advent

SAINT FRANCIS XAVIER

A native of Spain, Francis Xavier met St. Ignatius of Loyola while study-ing at the University of Paris. He became one of the first seven members of the Society of Jesus (the Jesuits). He was sent to preach the Gospel in the Orient. In ten years of missionary work, he brought more than 30,000 souls to the light of Christ. His travels took him to India and Japan, and he died on the doorstep of China. He is a patron saint of missions. He reminds us that the Gospel is meant for all people, and that every child is a child of God.

Preparation: *Come, Holy Spirit, enlighten the eyes of my heart.* Briefly review yesterday's prayer time (or the last time you prayed with *Oriens*, if you missed yesterday). Spend a minute being grateful for how God has been with you in your prayer time and indeed in all the moments of this week.

Lectio: In your own words ask God to help you wonder anew at the mar-vel, mystery, and miracle of his creation. The creation around us belongs to God. He has given it to us as a sacred trust. We exercise lordship over all creatures, but we ourselves are servants of the Lord. Read the passage slowly and prayerfully.

PSALM 8:2–10

> O Lord, our Lord,
>   how awesome is your name through all the earth!
> I will sing of your majesty above the heavens
>   with the mouths of babes and infants.
> You have established a bulwark against your foes,
>   to silence enemy and avenger.
> When I see your heavens, the work of your fingers,

the moon and stars that you set in place —
What is man that you are mindful of him,
   and a son of man that you care for him?
Yet you have made him little less than a god,
   crowned him with glory and honor.
You have given him rule over the works of your hands,
   put all things at his feet:
All sheep and oxen,
   even the beasts of the field,
The birds of the air, the fish of the sea,
   and whatever swims the paths of the seas.

O LORD, our Lord,
   how awesome is your name through all the earth!

Meditatio: There is only one God; how then can human beings be "little less than a god"? We have been made in the image and likeness of God. How has God crowned you with glory and honor? Have you used dominion over all creatures? Was God right to entrust you with his creation or have you proved less than trustworthy? Read the passage again slowly. Notice whatever word or phrase jumps out at you.

Oratio: God has not simply abandoned us or any other part of creation. Though we may not notice his quiet presence, he is always with us. The "babes and infants" do not recognize political correctness and tend to speak truth as they see it. God wants the same from us, his children. Speak to the Lord with child-like honesty. The Lord will listen patiently, so have no fear of not saying quite the right thing. Speak to him from your heart. When you are done, read the passage a third time.

Contemplatio: This time just be open to receive. Picture the heavens, the moon, and the stars, steady reminders of God's awesome power. How might God respond to what you have shared with him? Maybe it is a thought, word, or feeling. Just spend a few minutes letting God look at you with love, with you gazing back at him. Enjoy the presence of God before you move on.

SUGGESTIONS FOR JOURNALING

1. If I were to use my own words, I would say "crowned with glory and honor" means ...
2. I most marvel at creation when ...
3. I am most humbled by ...
4. I have experienced God's care when ...
5. I feel called to ...

After you've journaled, close with a brief conversation giving thanks to God for your prayer experience. You may be tempted to skip this as you've *already* talked to God. But keep in mind that the goal of prayer is not to have nice notes in a journal, but to have a deeper encounter with the God who loves you. So, after praying, reflecting, and journaling, have one more little chat with God. Think of it like talking to a friend as you walk them out to their car after a nice visit. You thank them for their visit and their friendship, don't you? Spend a moment saying: "Thank you, God." Then pray an Our Father.

December 4 — Saturday
Saturday of the First Week of Advent

REVIEW

Preparation: *Come, Holy Spirit, enlighten the eyes of my heart.* Instead of spending time with a new passage, we will pray with the passages that most spoke to you in this past week. Saint Ignatius called this kind of prayer time a "repetition." The idea behind a repetition is not so much to do a prayer passage all over again, but to go back to the place you most noticed God's presence and felt loved by God. You return to that place in order to deepen the encounter and the conversation with God. Flip back through your past week's journal entries. Notice what emerged in the conversations. Here are some questions to help you:

1. The prayer time that I enjoyed most and got the most out of was …
2. The prayer time I really struggled with was … What made it hard for me?
3. Where did I notice the presence of God? What did his presence feel like, or how did it affect me?
4. What was God doing, saying, or giving me this week?
5. How did I respond to what God was doing?
6. I'm most grateful for …

7. Is there one clear image of God's loving presence that emerged from my prayer during this first week? Or was there a word, phrase, or message that really touched me?

Savor that image of God's loving presence. Rest there for a few minutes. Then thank God for today's prayer time and end with an Our Father.

Week Two

Imaginative Prayer

How did *lectio divina* go? If you found yourself struggling, here are a couple of thoughts.

First, don't try too hard. We often think we have to "do prayer right" in order to get something from God. When we put the burden on ourselves, we really aren't open to receive. And receiving isn't hard work. The work comes when we have to let go of our expectations that prayer happens when "I pray well." In reality, prayer is just noticing and focusing on the presence and action of God in your life. God is present and active all the time. He doesn't talk only during one little part of prayer, and he doesn't stop talking just because you ended your prayer time. Many people find that they receive an answer to their prayer during Mass or before bedtime or at some other moment during the day. The secret is to have an attitude of willingness to receive from God whenever he might be communicating with us.

Secondly, remember that the goal is not to have nice notes in your journal. The goal is quality time with the God who loves you. If you've spent any quality time with God this past week, you've done well. Be careful not to judge your prayer too much. Just be grateful for the first week.

And if you didn't pray at all last week, that's OK. Life gets away from us sometimes. Just pick up with today's prayer and start here.

This week we will learn a new prayer form called imaginative prayer. St. Ignatius of Loyola was the pioneer of this prayer form. He stumbled on it quite by accident. It changed his life, and he went on to use it to help change other people's lives.

Some people are skeptical of this prayer form. They fear it is just creating fantasy air castles. You certainly could do that, but that wouldn't be prayer time. Prayer is about connecting with the God who loves you and is present with you right now. Most of us are only vaguely aware of God's presence. We are much more aware of our current location in space and time, what happened yesterday, and what is on our calendar for today. These are passing things that we need to temporarily unplug from if we want to connect more deeply with God.

A good book or movie will take you out of the present moment for a while and move you to another place and time. In doing so, it can help you connect with something deeper: your own hopes and dreams, your fears, your potential, and what it means to be part of the human condition. In a similar way, imaginative prayer helps connect you with the deeper reality of God's loving presence that is silently behind and beyond all space and time. The goal is not a great imaginative moment, but simply an encounter with God who was present in the Bible moment and is present right here with you today. The imagination is only a conversation starter. Again, if you spend quality time with God, you have achieved your goal.

Grace of the Week: We are surrounded by God's creation. But we are also creatures, created by God the Father and made for a relationship with him. This week we will explore our fall from a relationship with God and into the deep darkness of sin and death. Pray for the grace to experience the pain of separation from God and a deeper longing for a relationship with God.

December 5 — Sunday
Second Sunday of Advent

Preparation: *Come, Holy Spirit, enlighten the eyes of my heart.* Turn back to yesterday and look at that image of God's loving care for you that emerged in your review time. Use your imagination to picture that moment again. Spend about a minute just resting in that experience and savoring the unconditional love with which God loves you.

Set the Scene: Read the passage below. As you do, set the scene in your mind. Picture the looks on the faces of the captives as they were *led away on foot by their enemies, wrapped in mourning and misery.* Then picture them carried on royal thrones, wrapped in justice and glory.

BARUCH 5:1–9
Jerusalem, take off your robe of mourning and misery;
    put on forever the splendor of glory from God:
Wrapped in the mantle of justice from God,
    place on your head the diadem
    of the glory of the Eternal One.
For God will show your splendor to all under the
        heavens;
    you will be named by God forever:
    the peace of justice, the glory of God's worship.

Rise up, Jerusalem! stand upon the heights;
    look to the east and see your children
Gathered from east to west
    at the word of the Holy One,
    rejoicing that they are remembered by God.
Led away on foot by their enemies they left you:
    but God will bring them back to you
    carried high in glory as on royal thrones.
For God has commanded
    that every lofty mountain

and the age-old hills be made low,
That the valleys be filled to make level ground,
  that Israel may advance securely in the glory of
    God.
The forests and every kind of fragrant tree
  have overshadowed Israel at God's command;
For God is leading Israel in joy
  by the light of his glory,
  with the mercy and justice that are his.

Action! Read the passage a second time. What did the captives feel like and what did they experience as they waited to be rescued? Imagine God commanding that mountains be leveled and gorges filled in to make a smooth, easy return for them. What do they feel as they return to their homeland, thanking God that they are free at last?

Acknowledge: As you process this scene, notice what is happening in you. What thought or feeling resonates with you? What part of the passage is speaking to you?

Relate: Turn to God and share with him what is on your heart. This can be a more challenging part of the prayer. Think of it this way: You are watching the captives return when you notice someone standing next to you. You realize that God is with you, and he too is watching the scene. After watching for a while, turn and look at God. Let him look at you. Talk to him about what you noticed, thought, or felt.

Receive: What was in God's heart when his Spirit commanded the Prophet Baruch to write this passage? What is in God's heart for you? Receive whatever it is that God wants to give you — his thoughts, feelings, and desires. Read the passage a third time, or perhaps just the part that you feel most drawn to. As you do, focus on God and let him speak to you, or just quietly receive what he wants to give you.

Respond: Now answer him again. Respond to what you have received. Just be with the Lord and savor his loving presence for a minute or two before moving on.

SUGGESTIONS FOR JOURNALING

1. While imagining the scene, what stood out to me was …
2. When God entered the scene, I felt …
3. I sensed God communicating to me …
4. I have felt like a captive when …
5. I find the most joy when …

After you've journaled, close with a brief conversation giving thanks to God for your prayer experience. Then pray an Our Father.

December 6 — Monday
Monday of the Second Week of Advent

SAINT NICHOLAS, BISHOP

Saint Nicholas was the bishop of Myra in modern-day Turkey. He died on this day around AD 350. He is one of the most popular Christian saints, though very little is known about him. He is a patron of mariners, merchants, bakers, travelers, and children. There are many legends associated with him, one of which is that he brings little gifts to children on his feast day. He is known for his generosity. Ask him to help you experience more deeply the generosity of God that led him to create human beings.

Preparation: *Come, Holy Spirit, enlighten the eyes of my heart.* Call to mind a recent experience of God's loving care. Spend about a minute just resting in that experience and savoring the unconditional love with which God loves you. Let gratitude rise in your heart.

Set the Scene: In order to understand this passage, you have to understand how the ancient writers of the Bible saw the world. Picture a snow globe. It has a big dome over a heavy, stable base. Inside there are figures that experience snow when you shake the globe. Those figures are like us; we live inside the snow globe. Above our heads is a big blue dome called the sky (see Gn 1:6–8). The stars are like ceiling ornaments stuck inside the dome. The sun and moon travel up one side and down the other. The dome has big floodgates that open to let rain or snow fall on us. Beneath our feet is the underworld, and beneath it all is the abyss, a sort of endlessly deep ocean. God has his throne at the highest point of the dome. From there nothing escapes his view or his care. Try to picture God looking at you from his lofty throne as you read these words.

PSALM 33:13-22

*From heaven the L*ORD *looks down*
and observes the children of Adam,
From his dwelling place he surveys
all who dwell on earth.
The One who fashioned together their hearts
is the One who knows all their works.

A king is not saved by a great army,
nor a warrior delivered by great strength.
Useless is the horse for safety;
despite its great strength, it cannot be saved.
*Behold, the eye of the L*ORD *is upon those who fear him,*
upon those who count on his mercy,
To deliver their soul from death,
and to keep them alive through famine.

*Our soul waits for the L*ORD,
he is our help and shield.
For in him our hearts rejoice;
in his holy name we trust.
*May your mercy, L*ORD, *be upon us;*
as we put our hope in you.

Action! Read the passage a second time. Picture God gazing at you. Though he may seem distant, his all-seeing eye never misses a detail, and his steadfast love is ever present. God is more powerful than any king, or than all the powers of this world put together, for they are like toys that he himself made. He is like the boy who has created the model train set in the basement and planned every detail. God already sees the challenges you will face. He has already planned ahead to rescue you from them. Perhaps you can imagine yourself for a moment like one of the characters in the model train set, a character that is just noticing the maker, and realizing that the maker is looking at him with love. Read the passage a third time.

Acknowledge: How does it feel to know that God is gazing upon you with steadfast love? When have you trusted in God and he took care of you, delivered you from death and famine? Let your "heart be glad in him." Do you have any questions for God, or something you need to tell him?

Relate: Turn to God and share with him what is on your heart. Speak to God honestly, holding nothing back. Think of it like a conversation between a young child and his or her father.

Receive: How does God respond to your wonder, and your questions? What is in God's heart for you? Receive whatever it is that God wants to give you — a thought, a word, a feeling, or just a sense of wonder and awe. Read the passage a third time.

Respond: Now reply to what God has said or given you. Continue the conversation. When you're tired of talking, just be with the Lord for a minute or two before moving on.

SUGGESTIONS FOR JOURNALING
1. While praying with the scene, I pictured …
2. I was surprised to realize …
3. As God was gazing at me, I felt …
4. I struggled with …
5. I found myself wanting …

After you've journaled, close with a brief conversation giving thanks to God for your prayer experience. Then pray an Our Father.

December 7 — Tuesday

Tuesday of the Second Week of Advent

Preparation: *Come, Holy Spirit, enlighten the eyes of my heart.* Call to mind your recent experience of God's loving care. Spend about a minute just resting in that experience and savoring the unconditional love of the Father for his child. Let gratitude rise in your heart.

Set the Scene: God created Adam and placed him in the Garden of Eden. He gave him dominion over all the animals and let Adam name them all. But none proved to be a suitable partner for him. So, God put him to sleep and took out a rib from his side and formed it into a woman. What more could God have given them? Picture them in a beautiful garden surrounded by plants and animals of every kind. Yet they turn to the one thing God commanded them not to eat. Ask God for the grace to experience the pain of separation from him and a deeper longing for a relationship with God. Read through the passage and set the scene in your mind.

GENESIS 3:1–8

Now the snake was the most cunning of all the wild animals that the LORD God had made. He asked the woman, "Did God really say, 'You shall not eat from any of the trees in the garden'?" The woman answered the snake: "We may eat of the fruit of the trees in the garden; it is only about the fruit of the tree in the middle of the garden that God said, 'You shall not eat it or even touch it, or else you will die.'" But the snake said to the woman: "You certainly will not die! God knows well that when you eat of it your eyes will be opened and you will be like gods, who know good and evil." The woman saw that the tree was good for food and pleasing to the eyes, and the tree was desirable for gaining wisdom. So she took some of its fruit and ate it; and she also gave some to her husband, who was with her, and he ate it. Then the eyes of both of them were opened, and they knew that they were naked; so they sewed fig leaves together and made loincloths for themselves.

When they heard the sound of the LORD *God walking about in the garden at the breezy time of the day, the man and his wife hid themselves from the* LORD *God among the trees of the garden.*

Action! Read the passage a second time. Picture the delectable fruit, the cunning serpent, and the loss of innocence. What are Adam and Eve thinking? What are they feeling?

Acknowledge: What do you feel as the scene unfolds in front of you? Have you ever been guilty of taking things or doing things you knew you shouldn't do? Why did you do it? How did it feel?

Relate: Turn to God and share with him what is in your heart — your thoughts and feelings and desires. Read the passage a third time.

Receive: How does God respond to you? Just receive whatever God wants to give you — compassion, peace, conviction, or a new insight. Perhaps you have a hard time looking at God, or you are afraid of what God will say. Just let God look at you for a minute and share with him what you are afraid of.

Respond: Whatever it is that God has given you, respond to it. God already knows everything you've done. You can't hide from him. So, come out from the bushes and be with him for a few minutes before moving on.

SUGGESTIONS FOR JOURNALING
1. Before eating from the tree, the fruit looked …
2. After eating from the tree, this is what I noticed or realized …
3. Temptation and disappointment go hand in hand. When was I most tempted to break God's law, and most disappointed

with the results when I did break it?
4. My strongest thought, feeling, or desire was ...
5. I received a new insight or understanding ...

After you've journaled, close with a brief conversation giving thanks to God for your prayer experience. Then pray an Our Father.

December 8 — Wednesday

Solemnity of the Immaculate Conception

The Christian Church has long believed that the Blessed Virgin Mary was preserved free from all sin starting at the very moment of her conception. Christians have celebrated this feast for more than 1,200 years, but it was officially declared a dogma by Bl. Pope Pius IX in 1854. Four years later, Our Lady appeared to Saint Bernadette at Lourdes, France, and told her, "I am the Immaculate Conception." Today's feast is a holy day of obligation for Catholics, and the Gloria is sung at Mass.

Preparation: *Come, Holy Spirit, enlighten the eyes of my heart.* Call to mind your recent experience of God's loving care. Spend about a minute just resting in that experience and savoring the unconditional love of the Father for his child. Let gratitude rise in your heart.

Set the Scene: Ask God in your own words to experience the pain of separation from him. The Bible tells us that God would come walking in the garden at the breezy time of day (shortly before sunset in the area that is now Israel). He is surveying his property and visiting his favorite creatures. But not all is well today. Instead of coming to meet him, Adam and Eve hide themselves among the trees of the garden. Picture the scene in your mind as you read through this passage.

GENESIS 3:9–15, 20

The LORD God then called to the man and asked him: Where are you? He answered, "I heard you in the garden; but I was afraid, because I was naked, so I hid." Then God asked: Who told you that you were naked? Have you eaten from the tree of which I had forbidden you to eat? The man replied, "The woman whom you put here with me — she gave me fruit from the tree, so I ate it." The LORD God then asked the woman: What is

this you have done? The woman answered, "The snake
tricked me, so I ate it."
Then the LORD God said to the snake:

Because you have done this,
    cursed are you
    among all the animals, tame or wild;
On your belly you shall crawl,
    and dust you shall eat
    all the days of your life.
I will put enmity between you and the woman,
    and between your offspring and hers;
They will strike at your head,
    while you strike at their heel.

The man gave his wife the name "Eve," because she was
the mother of all the living.

Action! Read the passage again and let it unfold in your imagination. Notice each of the main actors in this drama. What motivates each of their actions?

Acknowledge: How does it feel for Adam to be caught red-handed, naked and afraid of God? When have you felt guilty, ashamed, naked? Are there feelings, or perhaps the memory of an experience, that reading this passage stirs up inside of you? Or if nothing personal comes to mind, imagine how Adam and Eve would have felt. Notice your strongest thought, feeling, or desire.

Relate: God is with you right here and right now. There is no need to be afraid of him or hide from him. Turn your heart to God. Speak to him in your heart. Share with him what this passage stirred up within you. Sometimes the biggest feeling might be that we don't want to share our feelings with God. Can you tell God that?

Receive: Read the passage a third time. How did God feel as the man and the woman hid from him? This time receive whatever is in God's heart for you: his thought, feeling, desire. If you find yourself struggling, know that you don't have to try so hard. Just be open to receive. Many times God gives something simple like a feeling of peace, a sense of his presence, or a sense that he understands what we are going through.

Respond: Receive what God has to give you, then answer him again. It may be just a simple "Thank you." Or it may stir up more to talk about. Perhaps you enter into a little conversation. Enjoy the presence of God for a minute or two before moving on.

SUGGESTIONS FOR JOURNALING
1. When I read this passage, what jumped out at me was …
2. My strongest thought, feeling, or desire was …
3. I saw with new eyes …
4. I ended prayer wanting …

After you've journaled, close with a brief conversation giving thanks to God for your prayer experience. Then pray an Our Father.

December 9 — Thursday
Thursday of the Second Week of Advent

SAINT JUAN DIEGO

On this day in 1531, a native Aztec man was on his way to Mass when he heard a voice calling to him. A beautiful woman was standing on the hill of Tepeyac near present-day Mexico City. She told him she was the ever-virgin mother of the true God and sent him to the bishop to ask for a church to be built on that spot so she could manifest her love for all people. The bishop was skeptical and sent Juan Diego back to ask the lady for a sign. On December 12, he returned and unfolded his mantle. Castilian roses fell out of the mantle. But even more surprisingly, a miraculous image of the lady herself appeared on his mantle. Millions of conversions followed this miracle. The image hangs today in the shrine of Our Lady of Guadalupe, testifying to her love for all people, including you.

Preparation: *Come, Holy Spirit, enlighten the eyes of my heart.* Call to mind an image of God's loving care for you that has emerged in your prayer. Spend about a minute just resting in that experience and savoring the unconditional love with which God loves you. Let gratitude rise in your heart. Then ask God in your own words to experience the pain of separation from him and a deeper longing for him.

Set the Scene: The story continues from yesterday. Adam and Eve stand before God wearing loin cloths of fig leaves that they had sewed together. Like a just judge, God is passing sentence on them.

GENESIS 3:16-19

To the woman he said:

    I will intensify your toil in childbearing;
    in pain you shall bring forth children.

> Yet your urge shall be for your husband,
> and he shall rule over you.

> To the man he said: Because you listened to your wife
> and ate from the tree about which I commanded you, You
> shall not eat from it,

> Cursed is the ground because of you!
> In toil you shall eat its yield
> all the days of your life.
> Thorns and thistles it shall bear for you,
> and you shall eat the grass of the field.
> By the sweat of your brow
> you shall eat bread,
> Until you return to the ground,
> from which you were taken;
> For you are dust,
> and to dust you shall return.

Action! Read the passage a second time. Picture every generation of women panting in pain as they struggle to bring life into the world. Picture generations of men fighting with thorns and thistles and plows, sweating for the food their families desperately need for survival. In the end, whether in childbirth or as a child or in old age, they all die. Their family digs a grave and recites, "For you are dust, and to dust you shall return" over an unbroken succession of graves and coffins and burial grounds.

Acknowledge: Adam and Eve are sentenced to hard labor — for her, the labor of bearing children; for him, the labor of tilling the earth. Because of Adam and Eve, men and women continue to toil and labor. Raising children, buying Christmas gifts, figuring out a way to pay for them all … feel the heaviness of the sentence that will rest on all human beings for all future generations. And lest we claim innocence, we have all sinned and fallen short of the glory of God, and we have each added to the burden of sin that weighs down humanity. When do you feel this burden weighing heavily upon you? What is your strongest thought, feeling, or desire?

Relate: God is with you right here and right now. Turn your heart to God. Speak to him in your heart. Share with him the burdens that you carry.

Receive: Remember that God is more than a judge. He is a Father deeply grieved by his children's sinfulness. He starts to unfold a plan to remedy their sinfulness. Christians have long believed that Jesus' death forgave even Adam and Eve, and that God took them to heaven in the end. Read the passage a third time. This time receive whatever is in God's heart for you: his thoughts, feelings, or desires. He loves you and is with you in the midst of your burdens. He desires to remedy sin and to help you carry this burden. Just be open to receive, without fear or expectation.

Respond: Receive what God wants to give you, then answer him back. It may be just a simple "Thank you." It may be a feeling of peace or a realization that you are not alone. Converse with the Lord for a minute or two and then spend a few minutes savoring his merciful love.

SUGGESTIONS FOR JOURNALING
1. My strongest thought, feeling, or desire was …
2. I feel burdened when …
3. I see the love of God in a new way …
4. I sensed God communicating to me …
5. A new insight or understanding I received was …

After you've journaled, close with a brief conversation giving thanks to God for your prayer experience. Then pray an Our Father.

December 10 — Friday

Friday of the Second Week of Advent

Preparation: *Come, Holy Spirit, enlighten the eyes of my heart.* Call to mind a recent experience of God's loving care. Spend about a minute just resting in that experience and savoring the unconditional love with which God loves you. Let gratitude rise in your heart.

Set the Scene: Ask God in your own words to let you experience the pain of separation from him and a deeper longing for a restored relationship. The Israelites are part of God's great project to rescue humanity from sin and death. They are meant to be a holy people, an example to the nations of what it looks like when we listen to God and follow his commandments. But instead, they have sunk into wickedness. Read the passage to set the scene.

ISAIAH 1:2–4,15–20

Hear, O heavens, and listen, O earth,
   for the LORD speaks:
Sons have I raised and reared,
   but they have rebelled against me!
An ox knows its owner,
   and an ass, its master's manger;
But Israel does not know,
   my people has not understood.
Ah! Sinful nation, people laden with wickedness,
   evil offspring, corrupt children!
They have forsaken the LORD,
   spurned the Holy One of Israel,
   apostatized.

When you spread out your hands,
   I will close my eyes to you;

Though you pray the more,
I will not listen.
Your hands are full of blood!
Wash yourselves clean!
Put away your misdeeds from before my eyes;
cease doing evil;
learn to do good.
Make justice your aim: redress the wronged,
hear the orphan's plea, defend the widow.

Come now, let us set things right,
says the LORD:
Though your sins be like scarlet,
they may become white as snow;
Though they be red like crimson,
they may become white as wool.
If you are willing, and obey,
you shall eat the good things of the land;
But if you refuse and resist,
you shall be eaten by the sword:
for the mouth of the LORD has spoken!

Action! You may find it hard to imagine this scene. It might help to call to mind recent news stories of bloodshed, mass shootings, and war. Every day there are thefts, frauds, sexual assaults, and murder perpetrated by people who are baptized into the family of God. Even clergy are guilty of monstrous crimes. These are the kind of scenes God is seeing as he speaks through the Prophet Isaiah. Read the passage again.

Acknowledge: Notice what it stirs up inside of you: thoughts, feelings, desires. Remember that God is a loving Father. It hurts him to see his children punished, but it hurts him more to see them doing evil. God wants his children to live good lives. If they refuse to turn from wickedness, he will be forced to punish them severely. It is right to be angry at the injustice around us. But are we not also guilty of tearing down our brothers and sisters, exploiting them or damaging their good name? The first victim of evil is always God himself.

Relate: Turn your heart to God and speak to him. Share with God what this passage stirred up within you. Now let him look at you with love. How does he respond?

Receive: Read the passage a third time. This time receive whatever is in God's heart for you — his thoughts, feelings, desires. How does it make God suffer when he sees his children hurting one another? What does he want for his children? Don't think too hard about this step. Just notice what comes up in the prayer.

Respond: Receive what God has to give you. Then respond in some way. Perhaps you need to say, "I'm sorry." Perhaps God is inviting you to some kind of action. Be with the Lord for a minute or two before moving on.

SUGGESTIONS FOR JOURNALING
1. A new insight or understanding I received was …
2. I felt convicted that …
3. I sensed God communicating to me …
4. I see sin in a new and different light …
5. I feel the Spirit of God moving me to a new way of acting, responding, or thinking …

After you've journaled, close with a brief conversation giving thanks to God for your prayer experience. Then pray an Our Father.

December 11 — Saturday
Saturday of the First Week of Advent

REVIEW

Preparation: *Come, Holy Spirit, enlighten the eyes of my heart.* Flip back through your past week's journal entries. As you do, notice what emerged in the conversation. Let gratitude rise in your heart. Here are some questions to help you:

1. Where did I notice God, and what was he doing or saying?
2. How did I respond to what God was doing?
3. I really struggled with …
4. Prayer really seemed to click when …
5. I'm grateful for …
6. Now at the end of this Second Week of Advent, what new meaning or purpose is emerging from your Advent pilgrimage? Perhaps go back and look at your very first day's prayer time.

7. What one image of God's loving presence sticks with me most strongly?

Conclude by conversing with God about your week. **Acknowledge** what you have been experiencing. **Relate** it to him. **Receive** what he wants to give you. **Respond** to him. Then savor that image of God's loving presence and rest there for a minute or two. Close with an Our Father.

Week Three

Relational Prayer (ARRR)

How was imaginative prayer? Some people love it, and some people struggle with it. *Lectio divina* can be used with any Scripture passage. Imaginative prayer works best with passages that contain visuals and action. As we move forward, I'll use one or the other prayer form each day, depending on what I think fits with the passage. You don't have to follow my guidance. If you prefer one prayer form, you can use it all the time. It's your journey. But let me encourage you to push yourself and try to become comfortable with either prayer form.

The second half of imaginative prayer can stand on its own. We call this relational prayer or "A-R-R-R." This prayer form has four steps:

Acknowledge what is going on inside of you — your thoughts, feelings, and desires. **Relate**, or share with the Lord what is going on inside of you. **Receive** what God wants to give you. **Respond** to what the Lord just gave you.

You can use this prayer form to pray with experiences from everyday life. Let's say, for example, that I'm out shopping. I'm stressed and feeling behind, and I end up having a run-in with a rude clerk (or fellow shopper, customer service rep, a mean text from a mother-in-law, etc.). I'm left fuming. But instead of nurturing feelings of bodily harm against this miserable human being, I can pray.

First, I need to start, as in all prayer, with calling to mind God's loving care for me and spending a minute resting in the free, unearned gift of loving and being loved. Then I notice what is going on inside of me. I don't want to consider only how I am feeling, but why I am feeling that way. What was the nerve that this encounter touched? How did what happened or what was said make me feel? There's always a feeling before we get angry, and that can be a key to understanding why I got angry or frustrated or hurt.

I turn to the God who loves me. I pour out my hurt, pain, and anger to God. The key with relating is that I need to shift my attention to God. First, I'm looking at myself and my problem. Then I share, and God listens, and God and I are looking at it together. Now I shift my attention so I am looking at God, and he is looking at me. How does he respond to what I have shared? Yes, he cares, but he has a different perspective. I want to receive his thoughts, feelings, or perspective. Maybe he gives me a new insight about my sensitivity, or perhaps a compassion for the things going on in this person's life. God's insight or perspective allows me to put this moment in perspective, and to see it with fresh eyes.

You might be surprised how much it will transform your perspective. Sharing your burdens with God makes them shrink like snow in the sunshine. It's almost like magic, but better. We call it grace. Practice this form of prayer with the experiences of your everyday life.

Grace of the Week: God has a plan to restore creation and undo the effects of sin. We need a savior, and God has just the thing. Pray for the grace of a deepening desire for God and a willingness to wait patiently until his plans for you unfold in their fullness.

December 12 — Sunday
Third Sunday of Advent

Preparation: *Come, Holy Spirit, enlighten the eyes of my heart.* Be present to the God who is always present to you. Call to mind his loving care for you and spend the first minute of your prayer just resting in the free, unearned gift of loving and being loved. Let gratitude rise in your heart.

Set the Scene: Ask God in your own words to give you a deepening desire for him and the grace to wait patiently until his plans unfold in their fullness. Read the passage for the first time and set the scene in your mind. John was clothed in camel's hair and ate locusts and wild honey. He is out in the wilderness preaching repentance. Crowds are gathering along the bank of the Jordan River to be baptized by him. Spend a few minutes building the scene in your imagination. What does the wilderness look like, feel like, smell like? Picture the mass of people coming to John to repent of their sins.

LUKE 3:10–18

And the crowds asked him, "What then should we do?" He said to them in reply, "Whoever has two tunics should share with the person who has none. And whoever has food should do likewise." Even tax collectors came to be baptized and they said to him, "Teacher, what should we do?" He answered them, "Stop collecting more than what is prescribed." Soldiers also asked him, "And what is it that we should do?" He told them, "Do not practice extortion, do not falsely accuse anyone, and be satisfied with your wages."

Now the people were filled with expectation, and all were asking in their hearts whether John might be the Messiah. John answered them all, saying, "I am baptizing you with water, but one mightier than I is coming. I am not worthy to loosen the thongs of his sandals. He

*will baptize you with the holy Spirit and fire. His winnow-
ing fan is in his hand to clear his threshing floor and to
gather the wheat into his barn, but the chaff he will burn
with unquenchable fire." Exhorting them in many other
ways, he preached good news to the people.*

Action! After you have spent some time picturing the scene, read the
passage a second time. John isn't sharing secret knowledge or giving
them complicated tasks. He's simply calling them back to honesty, generosity, and treating others fairly. We know right from wrong; we just find
excuses to do what we know is wrong. What might John say to you?

Place yourself in the scene. The "one mightier than I" is somewhere in
the crowd. Scan the crowd; do you notice him anywhere? What strikes
you about the Christ?

Acknowledge: Notice your strongest thought, feeling, or desire. What
is emerging inside of you as you are called to repentance and expect the
coming Messiah?

Relate: The long-awaited Messiah is next to you, standing or sitting
with you in the scene. He has come here for you. How does that make
you feel? Share with him what is on your heart. Let him look at you
with love. How does he respond?

Receive: Read the passage a third time. Receive whatever is in God's
heart for you — his thoughts, feelings, desires.

Respond: Now answer him back again. Just be with the Lord for a minute or two before moving on.

SUGGESTIONS FOR JOURNALING
1. While imagining the scene, what stood out to me was ...
2. When Jesus entered the scene, I felt ...
3. I sensed God communicating to me ...
4. I feel God calling me to a new way of thinking or acting ...

After you've journaled, close with a brief conversation, giving thanks to God for your prayer experience. Then pray an Our Father.

December 13 — Monday
Monday of the Third Week of Advent

Saint Lucy

Little is known about this young Christian girl from Syracuse in Sicily. It is said that a disappointed suitor denounced her as a Christian and she was executed in AD 304. She is one of just seven women mentioned by name in the Roman Canon (Eucharistic Prayer I) of the Mass. Her name comes from the Latin word *lux* meaning light. Because of this, she is a patroness of eyesight. Her feast day is celebrated with the lighting of candles, particularly in Scandinavian countries. Pray that God will enlighten your eyes and help make you a light to others.

Preparation: *Come, Holy Spirit, enlighten the eyes of my heart.* Call to mind God's loving presence and spend the first minute of your prayer just resting in the free, unearned gift of loving and being loved.

Lectio: Ask God in your own words to give you a deepening desire for him and the grace to wait patiently until his plans unfold in their fullness. Jeremiah is called to be a prophet during a difficult time when Israel is caught up in the wars of its more powerful neighbors, Egypt, Assyria, and Babylon. The kings waffle between the various factions to their own detriment. And more fundamentally, they often waffle between Yahweh and the worship of false gods. Read the passage slowly and prayerfully.

JEREMIAH 23:1–6

Woe to the shepherds who destroy and scatter the flock of my pasture — oracle of the LORD. Therefore, thus says the LORD, the God of Israel, against the shepherds who shepherd my people: You have scattered my sheep and driven them away. You have not cared for them, but I will take care to punish your evil deeds. I myself will gather the remnant of my flock from all the lands to which I have banished them and bring them back to their folds; there they shall be fruitful and multiply. I will raise up shepherds for them who will shepherd them so that they need no longer fear or be terrified; none shall be missing —oracle of the LORD.

> *See, days are coming — oracle of the LORD —*
> *when I will raise up a righteous branch for David;*
> *As king he shall reign and govern wisely,*
> *he shall do what is just and right in the land.*
> *In his days Judah shall be saved,*
> *Israel shall dwell in security.*
> *This is the name to be given him:*
> *"The LORD our justice."*

Meditatio: God means to step in. He will rescue the flock and raise up better shepherds. But this is not enough; God means to raise up a successor to King David who will bring justice and salvation. Jeremiah could not have known that it would take more than six hundred years for this prophecy to be fulfilled, or that the future king would be none other than the Son of God. What word or passage stands out to you? Read the passage a second time.

Oratio: God knows when you feel lost and scattered. He knows the struggles of enduring poor leadership from both political and religious leaders. He has plans to fulfill the desires of your heart. But what is it you desire? Open your heart and speak to God. Then read the passage a third time.

Comtemplatio: Now let him look at you with love. Receive whatever is in God's heart for you — his thoughts, feelings, desires, the plans he has to answer the yearnings in your heart. Just be with the Lord for a minute or two and bask in his loving care before moving on.

SUGGESTIONS FOR JOURNALING
1. I find myself struggling with …
2. I sensed God communicating to me …
3. I have a hard time accepting that …

4. My deepest desire right now is for …
5. I feel the Spirit of God moving me to a new way of acting, responding, or thinking …

S

After you've journaled, close with a brief conversation giving thanks to God for your prayer experience. Then pray an Our Father.

December 14 — Tuesday
Tuesday of the Third Week of Advent

Preparation: *Come, Holy Spirit, enlighten the eyes of my heart.* Be present to the God who is always present to you. Call to mind his loving care for you and spend the first minute of your prayer just resting in the free, unearned gift of loving and being loved. Let gratitude rise in your heart.

Lectio: Pray for the grace of a deepening desire for God and a confidence that his plans are better than your plans, and they are worth waiting for. Read the passage. As you do, think of what it would be like to be a citizen in this kingdom.

PSALM 72:2, 6-14

O God, give your judgment to the king;
  your justice to the king's son;
That he may govern your people with justice,
  your oppressed with right judgment,

May he be like rain coming down upon the fields,
  like showers watering the earth,
That abundance may flourish in his days,
  great bounty, till the moon be no more.

May he rule from sea to sea,
  from the river to the ends of the earth.
May his foes kneel before him,
  his enemies lick the dust.
May the kings of Tarshish and the islands bring tribute,
  the kings of Sheba and Seba offer gifts.
May all kings bow before him,
  all nations serve him.

For he rescues the poor when they cry out,
the oppressed who have no one to help.
He shows pity to the needy and the poor
and saves the lives of the poor.
From extortion and violence he redeems them,
for precious is their blood in his sight.

Meditatio: Whom do you serve? Do you want to be the king yourself? Do you run after those who look powerful, popular, or who offer promises? Or do you trust in God to lead you and guide you? All the kings fall down before this king; all the nations serve him. Do you serve him? Read the passage again.

Oratio: What do you really want from him? Speak to the king who offers righteousness and justice. He cares for the poor who call out to him. So, call out to him! If you have felt trampled or felt the sting of injustice, tell him about it. If you have been the one trampling others, turn to him and ask for mercy. Your blood is precious in his sight.

Contemplatio: Read the passage a third time. Now just receive what he wants to say to you or give you — a word, a phrase, an idea, a sense of peace, a new insight. Just be with this humble but mighty king for a few minutes.

SUGGESTIONS FOR JOURNALING
1. At this time of year I find myself a slave to ...
2. My deepest desire right now is for ...
3. He was inviting me to a new way of seeing, thinking, or acting ...
4. I ended prayer with a deeper sense of ...

After you've journaled, close with a brief conversation giving thanks to God for your prayer experience. Then pray an Our Father.

December 15 — Wednesday
Wednesday of the Third Week of Advent

Preparation: *Come, Holy Spirit, enlighten the eyes of my heart.* Remind your heart of God's loving presence and spend the first minute of your prayer just resting in the free, unearned gift of loving and being loved. Be grateful.

Set the Scene: Pray for the grace of a deepening desire for God and a willingness to wait patiently until his plans for you unfold in their fullness. Then read the passage. As you do, try to picture the blooming desert, the fearful, the blind, the lame and deaf. Use your imagination, but focus on the emotions.

ISAIAH 35:1–6

> The wilderness and the parched land will exult;
>   the Arabah will rejoice and bloom;
> Like the crocus it shall bloom abundantly,
>   and rejoice with joyful song.
> The glory of Lebanon will be given to it,
>   the splendor of Carmel and Sharon;
> They will see the glory of the LORD,
>   the splendor of our God.
> Strengthen hands that are feeble,
>   make firm knees that are weak,
> Say to the fearful of heart:
>   Be strong, do not fear!
> Here is your God,
>   he comes with vindication;
> With divine recompense
>   he comes to save you.
> Then the eyes of the blind shall see,
>   and the ears of the deaf be opened;

Then the lame shall leap like a stag,
and the mute tongue sing for joy.
For waters will burst forth in the wilderness,
and streams in the Arabah.

Action! Was there a particular word, phrase, or emotion that stood out to you? Read that part again. Or you can read the whole thing again. This time really savor the joy of God the Father in seeing so much joy and happiness.

Acknowledge: Notice what stirs up inside of you. What is your strongest thought, feeling, or desire?

Relate: Speak to God about what you are seeing, hearing, thinking, and feeling. Let him look at you with love. How does he respond? Read the passage one more time.

Receive: Receive whatever is in God's heart for you — his thoughts, feelings, desires.

Respond: Now answer him back again. Just be with the Lord for a minute or two before moving on.

SUGGESTIONS FOR JOURNALING
1. I have found the greatest joy on this Advent pilgrimage when …
2. A place in my life where I need healing is …
3. How does my hurt, wound, or struggle look differently if I know with confidence that the Father wants to heal me and will heal me?
4. I ended prayer wanting …

After you've journaled, close with a brief conversation giving thanks to God for your prayer experience. Then pray an Our Father.

December 16 — Thursday
Thursday of the Third Week of Advent

Preparation: *Come, Holy Spirit, enlighten the eyes of my heart.* Be present to the God who is always present to you. Call to mind his loving care for you and spend the first minute of your prayer just resting in the free, unearned gift of loving and being loved. Let gratitude rise in your heart.

Lectio: In your own words, ask God for the grace of a deepening desire for a relationship with him and a willingness to wait patiently as his plans for you fall into place. Zephaniah is a minor prophet who was active during the same time as Jeremiah. The book we have from him is just three short chapters, but they pack a punch. He opens with a scene of doom and destruction. The Lord will execute judgment on the nations and punish all evildoers. But despite the infidelities of Israel, God will spare a holy remnant, which will finally enjoy peace. This third week of Advent, what do you find is stealing your peace? Read the passage slowly and prayerfully.

ZEPHANIAH 3:12–18

> But I will leave as a remnant in your midst
>   a people humble and lowly,
> Who shall take refuge in the name of the LORD —
>   the remnant of Israel.
> They shall do no wrong
>   and speak no lies;
> Nor shall there be found in their mouths
>   a deceitful tongue;
> They shall pasture and lie down
>   with none to disturb them.
> Shout for joy, daughter Zion!
>   sing joyfully, Israel!

Be glad and exult with all your heart,
   daughter Jerusalem!
The LORD has removed the judgment against you,
   he has turned away your enemies;
The King of Israel, the LORD, is in your midst,
   you have no further misfortune to fear.
   On that day, it shall be said to Jerusalem:
Do not fear, Zion,
   do not be discouraged!
The LORD, your God, is in your midst,
   a mighty savior,
Who will rejoice over you with gladness,
   and renew you in his love,
Who will sing joyfully because of you,
   as on festival days.

I will remove disaster from among you,
   so that no one may recount your disgrace.

Meditatio: What misfortunes do you fear? What does it mean to take refuge in the name of the Lord? What word or phrase stands out to you? Read the passage again slowly.

Oratio: At this very moment, the Lord is in your midst. As always, he is listening to you. What struggles or fears are getting in the way of your prayer today? Speak to the Lord whatever is in your heart. When you are done sharing, read the passage a third time.

Contemplatio: What does God desire to give you? What is he calling you to? Spend a few minutes just receiving the loving gaze of God and being with him. Good prayer is really just quality time with God.

SUGGESTIONS FOR JOURNALING
1. My strongest thought, feeling, or desire was …
2. There was one particular fear that I noticed …
3. God was responding to me by …

4. I felt the love of God most strongly when …
5. The Good Shepherd is inviting me to …

After you've journaled, close with a brief conversation giving thanks to God for your prayer experience. Then pray an Our Father.

December 17 — Friday
Countdown to Christmas: Nine

O Wisdom of our God Most High,
guiding creation with power and love:
come to teach us the path of knowledge!

Nine days before Christmas, the Advent season switches gears. The lectionary gives us readings from the Gospel passages that immediately precede the birth of Jesus. Each day is assigned a special "O antiphon," a poetic invocation that draws on Old Testament prophecies to name who the coming Messiah is and what he will do. We will pray with the daily lectionary readings now until Christmas. These Gospel passages from Matthew and Luke will be familiar to you; perhaps you even prayed with them last year. As you pray with them again you will begin to see the genius of the liturgical year. God is, as Saint Augustine said, "Ever ancient, ever new." You have grown since last year's conversation with God. God will remind you of things from the past, but also guide you to new insights and experiences. Let's see what God has in store for you this year.

Preparation: *Come, Holy Spirit, enlighten the eyes of my heart.* Be present to the God who is always present to you. Call to mind his loving care for you and spend the first minute of your prayer just resting in the free, unearned gift of loving and being loved. Let gratitude rise in your heart.

Lectio: Pray for the grace of a deepening desire for God and a willingness to wait patiently until his plans for you unfold in their fullness. Read the passage slowly and prayerfully. Underline the names you recognize as you go along.

MATTHEW 1:1-17

The book of the genealogy of Jesus Christ, the son of David, the son of Abraham.

Abraham became the father of Isaac, Isaac the father of Jacob, Jacob the father of Judah and his brothers. Judah became the father of Perez and Zerah, whose mother was Tamar. Perez became the father of Hezron, Hezron the father of Ram, Ram the father of Amminadab. Amminadab became the father of Nahshon, Nahshon the father of Salmon, Salmon the father of Boaz, whose mother was Rahab. Boaz became the father of Obed, whose mother was Ruth. Obed became the father of Jesse, Jesse the father of David the king.

David became the father of Solomon, whose mother had been the wife of Uriah. Solomon became the father of Rehoboam, Rehoboam the father of Abijah, Abijah the father of Asaph. Asaph became the father of Jehoshaphat, Jehoshaphat the father of Joram, Joram the father of Uzziah. Uzziah became the father of Jotham, Jotham the father of Ahaz, Ahaz the father of Hezekiah. Hezekiah became the father of Manasseh, Manasseh the father of Amos, Amos the father of Josiah. Josiah became the father of Jechoniah and his brothers at the time of the Babylonian exile.

After the Babylonian exile, Jechoniah became the father of Shealtiel, Shealtiel the father of Zerubbabel, Zerubbabel the father of Abiud. Abiud became the father of Eliakim, Eliakim the father of Azor, Azor the father of Zadok. Zadok became the father of Achim, Achim the father of Eliud, Eliud the father of Eleazar. Eleazar became the father of Matthan, Matthan the father of Jacob, Jacob the father of Joseph, the husband of Mary. Of her was born Jesus who is called the Messiah.

Thus the total number of generations from Abraham to David is fourteen generations; from David to the Babylonian exile, fourteen generations; from the Babylonian *exile to the Messiah, fourteen generations.*

Meditatio: We often roll our eyes at the biblical genealogy because of the unpronounceable names. But these were real people who really lived. You may not know all these names, but God knows every single person on this list, and they are all precious to him. The remains of each one are buried somewhere here on earth, and God knows the resting place of them all. Some of them were famous saints and others were rather infamous. The lineage of the Messiah is just as messy as your family history and mine (read Genesis 38 if you doubt this). Yet God chose each link in an unbroken chain of ancestors that would give birth to his Son. All along, he was guiding creation with power and love. What does your bloodline look like? How might God be using you, and other ordinary people, to play a part in his extraordinary plans? Reflect for a few minutes, then read the passage again slowly, or just skim it and focus on whatever part of it spoke to you.

Oratio: Speak to God what is on your heart and mind. When you are done speaking, read the passage one more time, if you want to.

Contemplatio: Open your heart to receive what God wants to give you. Your life is a precious link in the chain of humanity. Receive whatever God wants to show you or give you: a word, image, or thought. But maybe you also will have a bit of a conversation. God is with you in this ordinary moment. Rest in and savor his love for you.

SUGGESTIONS FOR JOURNALING
1. I see God's hand in my own personal history when …
2. Because of my family or past, I struggle with …
3. I sensed God communicating to me …
4. I ended prayer wanting …
5. Optional: Write out your own genealogy after the style of this Scripture passage. Spend time praying for each of your ancestors.

After you've journaled, close with a brief conversation of thanksgiving to God for today's prayer time. Then pray an Our Father.

December 18 — Saturday
Countdown to Christmas: Eight

O Leader of the House of Israel,
giver of the Law of Moses on Sinai:
come to rescue us with your mighty power!

Preparation: *Come, Holy Spirit, enlighten the eyes of my heart.* Be present to the God who is always present to you. Call to mind his loving care for you and spend the first minute of your prayer just resting in the free, unearned gift of loving and being loved. Let gratitude rise in your heart.

Set the Scene: Ask for the grace to desire God and to say "Yes" to God's plans for you as they unfold in his time and in his wisdom. Read the passage. The betrothal of Mary and Joseph was a legal marriage. In accordance with the traditions of the time, young people married early and then prepared to live together. Joseph would have been preparing a place for his wife at his father's house. Picture the progress of this construction project; where was Joseph sleeping? Use your imagination to set the scene.

MATTHEW 1:18–25

Now this is how the birth of Jesus Christ came about. When his mother Mary was betrothed to Joseph, but before they lived together, she was found with child through the holy Spirit. Joseph her husband, since he was a righteous man, yet unwilling to expose her to shame, decided to divorce her quietly. Such was his intention when, behold, the angel of the Lord appeared to him in a dream and said, "Joseph, son of David, do not be afraid to take

Mary your wife into your home. For it is through the holy Spirit that this child has been conceived in her. She will bear a son and you are to name him Jesus, because he will save his people from their sins." All this took place to fulfill what the Lord had said through the prophet:

> *"Behold, the virgin shall be with child and bear a son, and they shall name him Emmanuel,"*

which means "God is with us." When Joseph awoke, he did as the angel of the Lord had commanded him and took his wife into his home. He had no relations with her until she bore a son, and he named him Jesus.

Action! Adultery was not only a sin, but it was also a crime, punishable by stoning to death. "Divorcing her quietly" would mean not denouncing her as an adulteress. It would mean, in essence, that the whole town thought Joseph was a deadbeat dad who had got his wife pregnant and then refused to live with her. It was God who gave the law that put Joseph in this predicament. Yet God will also show him a way through. God sees Joseph's willingness to sacrifice for his wife and invites him to a different form of sacrifice. What did it mean to Joseph to hear "God is with us" in his difficult situation? Read the passage again and let the scene unfold. What does Joseph experience through this dream? What does he think or feel? How does he act on the new information?

Acknowledge: Read the passage a third time. When have you been called to sacrifice? When has the presence of God helped you through a difficult conundrum? Notice your strongest thought, feeling, or desire.

Relate: Speak to God about what is on your heart. Let him look at you with love. How does he respond?

Receive: Receive whatever is in God's heart for you — his thoughts, feelings, desires.

Respond: Now answer him back again. Just be with the Lord for a minute or two before moving on.

SUGGESTIONS FOR JOURNALING

1. I found God in the midst of my struggles when …
2. My greatest fear or struggle seems to be …
3. I sensed God communicating to me …
4. I feel peace when …
5. God's love is inviting me to a new way of seeing, thinking, or acting today, as Christmas is now just one week away …

A Brief Review

We always pause on Saturdays for a little review of our week. Take a little time at the end of your prayer today and flip back through the previous week. Read these questions first and answer any of them that speak to you or help you focus on God's loving care for you.

1. How has God been present to me in the midst of the season's busyness?
2. Is there a particular theme that is emerging on my Advent pilgrimage?
3. What helps me stay present to God throughout the day, after my prayer time is done?
4. I find the greatest peace when …
5. During the final rush to Christmas, I desire most deeply …
6. The strongest image or moment of God's loving presence has been …

Acknowledge what you have been experiencing. **Relate** it to him. **Receive** what he wants to give you. **Respond** to him. Then savor that image of God's loving presence and rest there for a minute or two. Close with an Our Father.

Week Four

Making Prayer Happen When You Get Busy

Half an hour's meditation each day is essential, except
when you are busy. Then a full hour is needed.
— Saint Francis de Sales

It seems that my Advent always follows the same pattern. The first week or two, I find the season to be surprisingly enjoyable. I remark that I don't feel rushed this year and I look forward, finally, to a peaceful and prayerful Christmas. Then everything hits at once — Christmas cards start to pile up, time runs short, I realize I haven't sent any cards yet, I haven't bought gifts, and now last-minute planning for the Christmas season is upon me. My general habit is to freak out, get angry, and mutter under my breath, "I hate this season. Bah humbug!"

One year when I became so overwhelmed, I quit trying at all. I just sat in my prayer space and prayed a full, solid holy hour. I may have gone a few minutes over the hour; since I wasn't going to catch up, what difference did it make? Then I wandered over to the office and, to my surprise, accomplished far more than I ever thought possible. This is the paradox of prayer. When I focus on the work, instead of God, the work piles up. When I focus on God, instead of the work, the work gets done.

This is why I encourage you not to try to catch up if you miss a day. Or a week. Or are finally opening the book for the first time. *Oriens* shouldn't be yet another thing that piles up. Rather, I want you to see it as an invitation to quiet time with the Lord. When you approach it with the right attitude, you never really "fall behind" on *Oriens*.

One of the Devil's most successful temptations is to distract people for a day or two so they don't remember to pick up *Oriens*. Then when they finally remember to pray, the enemy whispers, "Oh well, you failed. You might as well give up now. You could try again next year." You wouldn't believe how many people fall for this little trick. There's also the daily trick: "I only have a few minutes now, so instead of praying I'll wait until later when I can pray it better." And of course, later never comes.

If you do fall a few days behind, do this: Read the Grace of the Week for the week you are on. Then turn to today's meditation and pray for today. You're all caught up! The goal is quality time with God, not getting every prayer prayed or making nice notes in your journal.

That having been said, the more you are able to open the book each day, the more you will benefit from the pilgrimage. Any prayer time in a day, however small, is a victory. Even just opening the book before bed and reading the Scripture passage for that day is a victory. We are on a prayer pilgrimage. If you just keep walking, even baby steps will eventually get you to your destination.

Grace of the Week: Let us open our hearts to our King, who humbled himself to free all men and women from sin, Satan, and death. Pray for a deeper awareness of the great mystery of Emmanuel, God with us.

December 19 — Sunday
Fourth Sunday of Advent

Countdown to Christmas: Seven

O Root of Jesse's stem,
sign of God's love for all his people:
come to save us without delay!

I chose the Scripture for today's meditation from the reading for the day (December 19) rather than for the Fourth Sunday of Advent. If you would prefer to meditate on the reading that will be read at today's Mass, turn ahead to Tuesday, December 21, and pray with Luke 1:39–45.

Preparation: *Come, Holy Spirit, enlighten the eyes of my heart.* Be present to the God who is always present to you. Call to mind his loving care for you and spend the first minute of your prayer just resting in the free, unearned gift of loving and being loved. Let gratitude rise in your heart.

Set the Scene: Ask God for a deeper awareness of Emmanuel, God with us, in your prayer time today. Read the passage. As you do, set the scene in your mind. We see an old priest going about his daily duties. What does the Temple look like? What does the angel look like? Picture the people outside waiting for Zechariah to emerge from the smoky, incense-filled Temple.

LUKE 1:5–25

In the days of Herod, King of Judea, there was a priest named Zechariah of the priestly division of Abijah; his wife was from the daughters of Aaron, and her name was Elizabeth. Both were righteous in the eyes of God, observing all the commandments and ordinances of the Lord blamelessly. But they had no child, because Elizabeth was barren and both were advanced in years. Once when he was serving as priest in his division's turn before God, according to the practice of the priestly service, he was chosen by lot to enter the sanctuary of the Lord to burn incense. Then, when the whole assembly of the people was praying outside at the hour of the incense offering, the angel of the Lord appeared to him, standing at the right of the altar of incense. Zechariah was troubled by what he saw, and fear came upon him. But the angel said to him, "Do not be afraid, Zechariah, because your prayer has been heard. Your wife Elizabeth will bear you a son, and you shall name him John. And you will have joy and gladness, and many will rejoice at his birth, for he will be great in the sight of [the] Lord. He will drink neither wine nor strong drink. He will be filled with the holy Spirit even from his mother's womb, and he will turn many of the children of Israel to the Lord their God. He will go before him in the spirit and power of Elijah to turn the hearts of fathers toward children and the disobedient to the understanding of the righteous, to prepare a people fit for the Lord." Then Zechariah said to the angel, "How shall I know this? For I am an old man, and my wife is advanced in years." And the angel said to him in reply, "I am Gabriel, who stand before God. I was sent to speak to you and to announce to you this good news. But now you will be speechless and unable to talk until the day these things take place, because you did not believe my words, which will be fulfilled at their proper time."

Meanwhile the people were waiting for Zechariah and were amazed that he stayed so long in the sanctuary. But when he came out, he was unable to speak to them, and they realized that he had seen a vision in the sanctuary. He was gesturing to them but remained mute. Then, when his days of ministry were completed, he went home. After this time his wife Elizabeth conceived, and she went into seclusion for five months, saying, "So has the Lord done for me at a time when he has seen fit to take away my disgrace before others."

Action! Read the passage a second time and play the scene forward in your mind. Today's antiphon is drawn from Isaiah 11:1–10. King David's line had long ago been "cut off" from royal power. But God would be raising up a new shoot from the "stump of Jesse" (King David's father), and "his dwellings shall be glorious." In a similar way, Zechariah and Elizabeth have long given up the dream of having their own child. Even though Zechariah is ministering in the Temple, the last thing he expects is for an angel to emerge from the clouds of incense. Even less is he prepared for the Good News the angel brings. What does he think or feel when the angel unexpectedly appears to him? How does he feel when he walks out of the Temple? How does Elizabeth feel?

Acknowledge: Even though you are praying and have connected with God in the past, do you doubt that God is present or will speak to you in a way you can understand? Is there a particular word, phrase, or moment that jumps out at you from this reading? What thoughts or feelings are stirred up by this reading? What is the desire of your heart?

Relate: Speak to God about the desires of your heart. Do you believe he is listening and will answer your prayers? Let him look at you with love. How does he respond?

Receive: Read the passage a third time and receive whatever is in God's heart for you — his thoughts, feelings, desires, his Good News for you. Do you believe that God can, and will, do good things in your life?

Respond: Continue the conversation. Enjoy God's loving presence with you in your current place of prayer before moving on.

SUGGESTIONS FOR JOURNALING
1. The thing that spoke to me most was …
2. I felt God stirring up a desire for …
3. I have a hard time trusting when …
4. My greatest fear or struggle seems to be …
5. I sensed God was with me and wanted me to know …

After you've journaled, close with a brief conversation giving thanks to God for your prayer experience. Then pray an Our Father.

December 20 — Monday
Monday of the Fourth Week of Advent

Countdown to Christmas: Six

O Key of David,
opening the gates of God's eternal kingdom:
come and free the prisoners of darkness!

Preparation: *Come, Holy Spirit, enlighten the eyes of my heart.* Be present to the God who is always present to you. Call to mind his loving care for you and spend the first minute of your prayer just resting in the free, unearned gift of loving and being loved. Let gratitude rise in your heart.

Set the Scene: Ask God for the grace of his loving presence with you, Emmanuel, to break into your daily life and take root in your heart. Read the passage through. Tradition usually sets the Annunciation at Mary's home in Nazareth. What time of day was it? Perhaps Mary has paused from her chores for a little prayer time. Use your imagination to set the scene.

LUKE 1:26–38

In the sixth month, the angel Gabriel was sent from God to a town of Galilee called Nazareth, to a virgin betrothed to a man named Joseph, of the house of David, and the virgin's name was Mary. And coming to her, he said, "Hail, favored one! The Lord is with you." But she was great-ly troubled at what was said and pondered what sort of greeting this might be. Then the angel said to her, "Do not be afraid, Mary, for you have found favor with God. Behold, you will conceive in your womb and bear a son, and you shall name him Jesus. He will be great and will be called Son of the Most High, and the Lord God will give him the throne of David his father, and he will rule over the house of Jacob forever, and of his kingdom there will be no end." But Mary said to the angel," How can this be, since I have no relations with a man?" And the angel said to her in reply, "The holy Spirit will come upon you, and the power of the Most High will overshadow you. Therefore the child to be born will be called holy, the Son of God. And behold, Elizabeth, your relative, has also conceived a son in her old age, and this is the sixth month for her who was called barren; for nothing will be impossible for God." Mary said, "Behold, I am the handmaid of the Lord. May it be done to me according to your word." Then the angel departed from her.

Action! Read the passage a second time and play the scene forward in your mind. Today's O antiphon takes the key of David (Is 22:22) in two different directions: It will open the kingdom of heaven that was closed by Eve's sin, and it will unlock the prisoners who have been kept in darkness by that same sin. But the key doesn't have the power to unlock Mary's womb; only she can do that. All of creation, groaning under the sentence of sin, awaits her answer with bated breath. What will she say? Will we finally have the long-awaited Savior that God has promised us?

Acknowledge: Read the passage a third time, or just the part that most speaks to you. Why is this virgin greatly troubled at the angel's words? What is in her heart at this moment? What does her "Yes" feel like for her? Notice what is going on inside of you. Do you sometimes have a hard time accepting God's plans for your life? Is God waiting for you to "unlock" your heart to him?

Relate: Speak to Mary about your thoughts and feelings. Together with her, turn to God in prayer. Share what is on your heart with complete honesty. Question God, as Mary questioned the angel. Don't hide your feelings from God.

Receive: Receive whatever is in God's heart for you — his thoughts, feelings, desires. He did all this for you. What more does he want to give you? If you have a hard time receiving, ask Mary to show you how to receive.

Respond: God wants to dwell in your heart as he dwelt in the womb of Mary. Cherish the gift of God's love, not only for you and with you, but even within you. Converse with God in your heart. Then just be with the Lord and with Mary for a minute or two before moving on.

SUGGESTIONS FOR JOURNALING

1. My heart is troubled by …
2. How have I responded when God's plans interrupted my plans?
3. God's presence feels like …
4. I sensed God was with me and wanted me to know …
5. I ended prayer wanting …

After you've journaled, close with a brief conversation with God giving thanks for your prayer experience. Then pray a Hail Mary.

December 21 — Tuesday
Countdown to Christmas: Five

O Radiant Dawn,
splendor of eternal light, sun of justice:
come and shine on those who dwell
in darkness and in the
shadow of death.

Preparation: *Come, Holy Spirit, enlighten the eyes of my heart.* Be present to the God who is always present to you. Call to mind his loving care for you and spend the first minute of your prayer just resting in the free, unearned gift of loving and being loved. Let gratitude rise in your heart.

Set the Scene: Ask for the grace to welcome Mary, the God-bearer, that your heart might leap for joy at the nearness of the promised Messiah, Emmanuel. Read the passage through. Tradition identifies this location as a town called Ein Karem, a hill town about five miles to the west of Jerusalem and about ninety miles from Nazareth. Elizabeth is already six months pregnant. Mary hasn't started to show yet.

LUKE 1:39–45

During those days Mary set out and traveled to the hill country in haste to a town of Judah, where she entered the house of Zechariah and greeted Elizabeth. When Elizabeth heard Mary's greeting, the infant leaped in her womb, and Elizabeth, filled with the holy Spirit, cried out in a loud voice and said, "Most blessed are you among women, and blessed is the fruit of your womb. And how does this happen to me, that the mother of my Lord should come to me? For at the moment the sound of your greet-

ing reached my ears, the infant in my womb leaped for joy. Blessed are you who believed that what was spoken to you by the Lord would be fulfilled."

Action! Read the passage a second time and play the scene forward in your mind. Emmanuel means "God with us" (Is 7:14). How was God with Mary on her journey to visit Elizabeth? How does Elizabeth feel in the presence of her infant Lord? How is God with you right now?

Acknowledge: Christmas is a busy time for visiting and receiving visitors. Do your visitors bring the presence of Jesus to your home, or do they bring worries of being judged for a messy home? When you visit others, how do you bring Jesus with you to their home? When did you leap for joy at God's presence in your life?

Relate: Let your thoughts and feelings rise to the surface. Speak to God what is in your heart.

Receive: Read the passage a third time. How does God the Father view this scene? How does he gaze upon your visits and visitors? Receive whatever is in God's heart for you — his thoughts, feelings, desires.

Respond: Converse with God in your heart. Then just savor the presence of Jesus for a minute or two before moving on.

SUGGESTIONS FOR JOURNALING
1. My heart leaped for joy when …
2. I sensed God saying to me …
3. I ended prayer wanting …
4. Is there a way I can "go in haste" to share with another the joy I am receiving through these Advent prayer times?

130 December 21 — Tuesday

After you've journaled, close with a brief conversation with God giving thanks for your prayer experience. Then pray a Hail Mary.

December 22 — Wednesday
Countdown to Christmas: Four

O King of all nations and keystone of the Church:
come and save man, whom you formed from the dust!

Preparation: *Come, Holy Spirit, enlighten the eyes of my heart.* Be present to the God who is always present to you. Call to mind his loving care for you and spend the first minute of your prayer just resting in the free, unearned gift of loving and being loved. Let gratitude rise in your heart.

Lectio: Ask in your own words that God might fill your heart with the joy of Emmanuel, God with us. Read the passage slowly and prayerfully. This Scripture is called the *Magnificat* (which is the first word of this passage in Latin). It is a hymn of praise to God who has been faithful to his promises from Abraham until today. This could very well be a song that the saints sing in heaven. Is there one word or phrase that you feel moved to focus on?

LUKE 1:46–56
And Mary said:

"My soul proclaims the greatness of the Lord;
my spirit rejoices in God my savior.
For he has looked upon his handmaid's lowliness;
behold, from now on will all ages call me blessed.
The Mighty One has done great things for me,
and holy is his name.
His mercy is from age to age
to those who fear him.
He has shown might with his arm,

dispersed the arrogant of mind and heart.
He has thrown down the rulers from their thrones
but lifted up the lowly.
The hungry he has filled with good things;
the rich he has sent away empty.
He has helped Israel his servant,
remembering his mercy,
according to his promise to our fathers,
to Abraham and to his descendants forever."

Mary remained with her about three months and then returned to her home.

Meditatio: Have you noticed recent news stories where God was humbling the proud or lifting up the lowly? How has God done great things for you? Have you experienced his mercy, blessing, or strength? Or perhaps you feel lowly, humbled, someone who needs to be raised from the dust, and you are waiting for the King of all nations to come rescue you with the might of his arm. Reflect for a few minutes or just focus on the word or phrase that speaks to you. Then read the passage again slowly.

Oratio: Speak to God what is on your heart and mind, your thoughts, feelings, and desires. When you are done speaking, read the passage one more time.

Contemplatio: Open your heart to receive what God wants to give you. Maybe it is a thought, a word, or a sense of peace. God is with you in this ordinary moment. Even his challenging words come with love. Rest in and savor his love for you. Be present. Be lowly.

SUGGESTIONS FOR JOURNALING
1. My favorite word or phrase was …
2. God fulfilled his promises to me when …
3. I rejoice in God my savior when I recall …
4. The people and the world around me most need to hear …

5. Mary takes Jesus with her wherever she goes. How can I take Jesus with me on my journey today?

After you've journaled, close with a brief conversation with God giving thanks for your prayer experience. Then close by reading today's Scripture one more time as a prayer of praise and thanksgiving.

December 23 — Thursday
Countdown to Christmas: Three

O Emmanuel, our King and Giver of Law:
come to save us, Lord our God!

Preparation: *Come, Holy Spirit, enlighten the eyes of my heart.* Be present to the God who is always present to you. Call to mind his loving care for you and spend the first minute of your prayer just resting in the free, unearned gift of loving and being loved. Let gratitude rise in your heart.

Set the Scene: Ask God for the grace to see Emmanuel, God with us, in the lives of your friends and relatives. It's easy to imagine Elizabeth's neighbors and relatives gathering around to celebrate the birth of a healthy baby boy. The circumcision was like a baptism party. The name John means "God is gracious." Set the scene in your imagination. Populate it with villagers.

LUKE 1:57–66

When the time arrived for Elizabeth to have her child she gave birth to a son. Her neighbors and relatives heard that the Lord had shown his great mercy toward her, and they rejoiced with her. When they came on the eighth day to circumcise the child, they were going to call him Zechariah after his father, but his mother said in reply, "No. He will be called John." But they answered her, "There is no one among your relatives who has this name." So they made signs, asking his father what he wished him to be called. He asked for a tablet and wrote, "John is his name," and all were amazed. Immediately his mouth was opened, his tongue freed, and he spoke blessing God. Then fear came upon all their neighbors, and all these matters were discussed throughout the hill country of Judea. All who heard these things took them to heart, saying, "What, then, will this child be?" For surely the hand of the Lord was with him.

Action! Read the passage a second time and play the scene forward in your mind. See the looks on the faces of the guests and their excited conversation. Zechariah is only a silent participant — imagine the look on his face as he meets his son and welcomes his guests. Imagine the look on everyone's face when suddenly he can speak again! Even though Mary isn't mentioned, she was probably in the crowd somewhere — why else would she have remained for three months with Elizabeth? Place yourself within the crowd.

Acknowledge: Read the antiphon for today. How do you feel at the birth of this child who will prepare the way for the *King of all nations and keystone of the Church*? What thoughts and feelings rise in your heart?

Relate: Speak to God what is in your heart. If you have a hard time expressing yourself, maybe Zechariah can help.

Receive: Read the passage a third time and receive whatever is in God's heart for you — his thoughts, feelings, desires. Does your heavenly Father look at you like Zechariah looked at his son, John?

Respond: Let the Father look at you and look back at him. Just savor the joy of being your Father's child for a few minutes before moving on.

SUGGESTIONS FOR JOURNALING
1. I was surprised by …
2. Zechariah teaches me …
3. The Father seemed to be saying to me …
4. When do I feel tongue-tied, or when do I find it hard to speak to God? Or was there something today that I had a hard time receiving and accepting?
5. I ended prayer wanting …

After you've journaled, close with a brief conversation with God giving thanks for your prayer experience. Then pray a Hail Mary.

December 24 — Friday
Countdown to Christmas: Two

Preparation: *Come, Holy Spirit, enlighten the eyes of my heart.* Be present to the God who is always present to you. Call to mind his loving care for you and spend the first minute of your prayer just resting in the free, unearned gift of loving and being loved. Let gratitude rise in your heart.

Lectio: Ask for the grace to see Emmanuel, God with us, in your own history and in the present moment. Zechariah hasn't spoken for nine months — and now he has a lot to say! He proclaims that this child will brighten all the world and bring a freedom far greater than the Israelites experienced as they left Egypt. Read this passage slowly and prayerfully. Is there a word or phrase that speaks to you most strongly?

LUKE 1:67–79

Then Zechariah his father, filled with the holy Spirit, prophesied, saying:

"Blessed be the Lord, the God of Israel,
for he has visited and brought redemption to his
people.
He has raised up a horn for our salvation
within the house of David his servant,
even as he promised through the mouth of his holy
prophets from of old:
salvation from our enemies and from the hand of all
who hate us,
to show mercy to our fathers
and to be mindful of his holy covenant
and of the oath he swore to Abraham our father,

and to grant us that,
rescued from the hand of enemies,
without fear we might worship him
in holiness and righteousness
before him all our days.
And you, child, will be called prophet of the Most High,
for you will go before the Lord to prepare his ways,
to give his people knowledge of salvation
through the forgiveness of their sins,
because of the tender mercy of our God
by which the daybreak from on high will visit us
to shine on those who sit in darkness and death's shadow,
to guide our feet into the path of peace."

Meditatio: O Radiant Dawn! The dawn from on high that shall break upon us. You guessed it, that is the word *Oriens*. With this being the day before Christmas, it is as though the dawn is just starting to peak out over the hills. Have you felt God's light shining more brightly these last twenty-seven days? Has God been guiding your feet into the way of peace? Read the passage again, or maybe just the part that speaks to you.

Oratio: What do you want to say to God, with the birth of his Son so close at hand? Speak to God what is on your heart and mind. When you are done speaking, soak in the passage.

Contemplatio: Read the passage one more time, if you find that helpful. Open your heart to receive what God wants to give you. God loves every child like an only child. Rest in and savor his love for you. Let the dawn from on high shine upon you. Bask in the light of God's love for a few minutes before moving on.

SUGGESTIONS FOR JOURNALING
1. I see more clearly now ...
2. I more strongly desire ...
3. I need patience as I wait for ...

4. God's love feels like …
5. What I really want for Christmas is …

After you've journaled, close with a brief conversation with God giving thanks for your prayer experience. Then read today's Scripture one more time as a prayer of praise and thanksgiving.

The King Is Born

The text below, taken from the Roman martyrology, presents the birth of Jesus as one would announce the birth of a king or emperor. The announcement is recited or chanted on December 24, during the celebration of the Liturgy of the Hours or before the Christmas Mass during the night.

Let us prepare our hearts to celebrate the birth of our Savior. Come, Lord Jesus, into our hearts, our families, our world!

The Twenty-fifth Day of December, when ages beyond number had run their course from the creation of the world, when God in the beginning created heaven and earth, and formed man in his own likeness;

when century upon century had passed since the Almighty set his bow in the clouds after the Great Flood, as a sign of covenant and peace; in the twenty-first century since Abraham, our father in faith, came out of Ur of the Chaldees;

in the thirteenth century since the People of Israel were led by Moses in the Exodus from Egypt; around the thousandth year since David was anointed King;

in the sixty-fifth week of the prophecy of Daniel; in the one hundred and ninety-fourth Olympiad; in the year seven hundred and fifty-two since the foundation of the City of Rome;

in the forty-second year of the reign of Caesar Octavian Augustus, the whole world being at peace,

JESUS CHRIST, eternal God and Son of the eternal Father, desiring to consecrate the world by his most loving presence, was conceived by the Holy Spirit, and when nine months had passed since his conception, was born of the Virgin Mary in Bethlehem of Judah, and was made man:

The Nativity of Our Lord Jesus Christ according to the flesh.

Appendix 1 of the Roman Missal, Third Edition

December 25 — Saturday

The Nativity of Our Lord Jesus Christ

Preparation: *Come, Holy Spirit, enlighten the eyes of my heart.* Be present to the God who is always present to you. Call to mind his loving care for you and spend the first minute of your prayer just resting in the free, unearned gift of loving and being loved. Let gratitude rise in your heart.

Set the Scene: Pray for the grace to be caught up into the great mystery of Emmanuel, God with us. We like to think of the Nativity as something easy, peaceful, and cozy. But our Gospel implies crowds thronging to fulfill the decree, a long journey on dusty roads with a very pregnant woman, and finding yourself homeless at the most inopportune time. Read through the Gospel to set the scene in your imagination.

LUKE 2:1-20

In those days a decree went out from Caesar Augustus that the whole world should be enrolled. This was the first enrollment, when Quirinius was governor of Syria. So all went to be enrolled, each to his own town. And Joseph too went up from Galilee from the town of Nazareth to Judea, to the city of David that is called Bethlehem, because he was of the house and family of David, to be enrolled with Mary, his betrothed, who was with child. While they were there, the time came for her to have her child, and she gave birth to her firstborn son. She wrapped him in swaddling clothes and laid him in a manger, because there was no room for them in the inn.

Now there were shepherds in that region living in the fields and keeping the night watch over their flock. The angel of the Lord appeared to them and the glory of the Lord shone around them, and they were struck with great fear. The angel said to them, "Do not be afraid;

for behold, I proclaim to you good news of great joy that will be for all the people. For today in the city of David a savior has been born for you who is Messiah and Lord. And this will be a sign for you: you will find an infant wrapped in swaddling clothes and lying in a manger." And suddenly there was a multitude of the heavenly host with the angel, praising God and saying:

> *"Glory to God in the highest*
> *and on earth peace to those on whom his favor*
> *rests."*

When the angels went away from them to heaven, the shepherds said to one another, "Let us go, then, to Bethlehem to see this thing that has taken place, which the Lord has made known to us." So they went in haste and found Mary and Joseph, and the infant lying in the manger. When they saw this, they made known the message that had been told them about this child. All who heard it were amazed by what had been told them by the shepherds. And Mary kept all these things, reflecting on them in her heart. Then the shepherds returned, glorifying and praising God for all they had heard and seen, just as it had been told to them.

Action! Read the passage a second time and play the scene forward in your mind. Sometimes we find ourselves trying to make a life for ourselves as world events swirl around us. Did Joseph and Mary know why they were making this journey? Did they perhaps fret about the destination and the challenge of finding housing? God provides an unorthodox, but effective, bed for his little Son. God "lifts up the lowly" by inviting humble shepherds to come and adore the newborn king. Where do you find yourself in this scene?

Acknowledge: Read the passage a third time. You are watching God fulfill his promise of mercy. What is in Mary's heart? Joseph's heart? The heart of the shepherds? Your heart?

Relate: Speak to God what is in your heart.

Receive: Receive whatever is in God's heart for you. Perhaps you can ask Mary to let you hold her child. What do you feel in your heart as you contemplate the Savior?

Respond: Just savor the joy of holding the Son and being held by the Father for a little while. Let God the Father gaze at you as you gaze on the face of his Son.

SUGGESTIONS FOR JOURNALING

1. The glory of the Lord shone in my Christmas celebration when …
2. I felt God's love most strongly …
3. What does it mean to say that the prophecies were meant for me, the Messiah was prepared for me, that Jesus was born for me?
4. The Father seemed to be saying to me …
5. I was surprised by …
6. My heart rested when …

_____

_____

_____

_____

_____

_____

_____

_____

_____

_____

_____

_____

_____

_____

_____

After you've journaled, pause to **Review** the last nine days, the whole Countdown to Christmas that began on Friday, December 17. Read these questions first and answer any of them that are helpful to you.

1. How has the countdown made Christmas Day a richer experience for me?
2. What was the biggest grace or gift I received from God on this pilgrim journey?
3. What birthday gift did I give baby Jesus?
4. The strongest image of God's love for me has been ...
5. I was most able to rest in God's love for me when ...

Acknowledge what you have been experiencing. **Relate** it to him. **Receive** what he wants to give you. **Respond** to him. Then savor that image of God's loving presence and rest there for a minute or two. Close with an Our Father.

Week Five

A Feast Fit for a King

The feast of Christmas is too big to fit into one day. For eight days we celebrate the long-awaited Radiant Dawn, the Sun of Justice and King all nations who is Christ the Lord. I tell schoolchildren that the Octave of Christmas means you have to eat Christmas treats every day for eight days. The Gloria is sung at Mass for all eight days of the octave. Some of these days are special feast days dedicated to particular saints.

During the octave, swap out the purple and pink candles on your Advent wreath for white candles. Light them when you eat your family meals and sing a Christmas carol together each time. And keep making time for your pilgrimage! We've come through Advent and have only begun to journey through Christmas.

Maybe you had the best of intentions but just forgot to pick up this book. That's OK! You can start praying again any time. Pilgrimages are never just a smooth road. On my five-day walking pilgrimages, the middle day is usually a Wednesday, and it is often the most challenging day for pilgrims. You might find reasons to give up, excuses not to pray, or you might say things like, "I'll just try again next year." Just because it wasn't the pilgrimage you wanted doesn't mean you've missed out on the journey that God planned for you. Do not be discouraged when you encounter various forms of resistance. If praying was hard for you, if you were tempted to give up, if you faced criticism from friends or family members, if you felt discouraged, or that you were "no good at praying"… good! Resistance is part of the journey. Overcoming resistance is an important part of growth in any area of our lives. If you encounter resistance, it is a sign that you are on the right road. Keep walking!

Do not be discouraged either if your *Oriens* pilgrimage hasn't yet been what you were perhaps expecting or hoping it would be. I went on a pilgrimage to the Holy Land. We visited the Sea of Galilee for a five-day retreat. It was the most dry and difficult retreat I've ever had. I got no fruit from any of the prayer times until after the retreat had technically ended. While it wasn't a particularly enjoyable retreat, I have never forgotten the lessons I learned from it.

Remember that prayer is really about spending time with the God who loves us. It's not about filling pages of a journal with amazing in-sights or experiences. You shouldn't compare our retreat with anyone else's. If you are open to an encounter, then God will come and meet you. Even if it hasn't looked exactly as you might have planned, quality time with God is always time well spent. We still have more than half our pil-grimage ahead of us. So, keep walking and let's see what awaits us around the next corner.

Grace of the Week: We continue to celebrate the Octave of Christmas. Our readings this week will be drawn from the daily Mass readings or the Scriptures for each feast day. Pray for a deeper sense of peace and joy in the birth of Jesus, and pray that his light will shine in the dark corners of your heart and your world.

December 26 — Sunday
The Holy Family of Jesus, Mary, and Joseph

Preparation: *Come, Holy Spirit, enlighten the eyes of my heart.* Be present to the God who is always present to you. Call to mind his loving care for you and spend the first minute of your prayer just resting in the free, unearned gift of loving and being loved. Let gratitude rise in your heart.

Set the Scene: Ask God for a deeper sense of joy and peace in the birth of Jesus, that his light will shine in the dark corners of your heart and your world. Read the passage through. The reading for today's feast day is the "finding of Jesus in the Temple" — baby Jesus sure grew up quickly! This passage is the only scriptural reference to Jesus' life between his infancy and the beginning of his public ministry. We don't often see this passage in the light of the Christmas story. Let's dig into it and see what it can tell us about Jesus' birth. As you read it, set the scene in your mind. Picture the chaos as many pilgrims arrive in Jerusalem (not unlike the census years earlier). At twelve years of age, Jesus is now mature enough to participate in this yearly custom for the first time. He probably spent a lot of time with the other boys his age, as well as relatives and acquaintances of his parents. So, his parents didn't notice his absence at first. We often think of the Holy Family posing in the manger scene, a perfect child and perfect parents. But apparently, even the Holy Family struggled sometimes.

LUKE 2:41–52

Each year his parents went to Jerusalem for the feast of Passover, and when he was twelve years old, they went up according to festival custom. After they had completed its days, as they were returning, the boy Jesus remained behind in Jerusalem, but his parents did not know it. Thinking that he was in the caravan, they journeyed for a day and looked for him among their relatives and acquaintances, but not finding him, they returned to Jerusalem to look for him. After three days they found him in the temple, sitting in the midst of the teachers, listening to them and asking them questions, and all who heard him were astounded at his understanding and his answers. When his parents saw him, they were astonished, and his mother said to him, "Son, why have you done this to us? Your father and I have been looking for you with great anxiety." And he said to them, "Why were you looking for me? Did you not know that I must be in my Father's house?" But they did not understand what he said to them. He went down with them and came to Nazareth, and was obedient to them; and his mother kept all these things in her heart. And Jesus advanced [in] wisdom and age and favor before God and man.

Action! Read the passage a second time and play the scene forward in your mind. See the huge Temple towering above the people and the solemn sacrifices being offered to the God of heaven and earth. Rather than being intimidated by it all, Jesus feels completely at home here. Picture the scene with the teachers. What do Mary and Joseph feel as they lose, and then find, the Son of God?

Acknowledge: Read the passage a third time. Place yourself in the scene. Focus on the part that speaks to you. What thoughts, feelings, and desires are rising in your heart?

Relate: Speak to God what is in your heart. Or wait until the end of the prayer time, as we have before with imaginative prayer, and have a conversation with the boy Jesus, his mother, Mary, or his father, Joseph.

Receive: Mary has pondered the Christmas events in her heart for many years. Ponder these events yourself and listen to what the Holy Spirit wants to reveal to you in today's prayer. Just receive for a few minutes.

Respond: You too are God's child, and the Temple is your Father's house. Just savor the light of the Holy Spirit shining on your heart and respond to whatever God is giving you.

SUGGESTIONS FOR JOURNALING

1. What struck me the most in today's reading was …
2. My family life looks different …
3. My strongest thought, feeling, or desire was …
4. I ended prayer wanting …
5. I saw Christmas in a new way …

After you've journaled, close with a brief conversation with God giving thanks for your prayer experience. Then pray an Our Father.

December 27 — Monday
Third Day in the Octave of Christmas

Saint John, Apostle and Evangelist

Born in Bethsaida, the brother of James and a fisherman by trade, John was called to follow Jesus while mending his nets at the Sea of Galilee. Along with his brother James and fellow fisherman Peter, he was present at the Transfiguration of the Lord. At the Last Supper, he reclined at table next to Jesus. He stood at the foot of the cross as Jesus died, and Jesus entrusted his mother to John's care. He is known as the "beloved disciple." John wrote the fourth Gospel, three epistles, and the Book of Revelation. The youngest of all the apostles, he was the only one not to be martyred. Tradition holds that he was miraculously preserved from attempts to kill him and was then exiled to the island of Patmos.

Preparation: *Come, Holy Spirit, enlighten the eyes of my heart.* Be present to the God who is always present to you. Call to mind his loving care for you and spend the first minute of your prayer just resting in the free, unearned gift of loving and being loved. Let gratitude rise in your heart.

Lectio: Ask God for a deeper sense of peace and joy in the birth of Jesus, that his light will shine in the dark corners of your heart and your world. Saint John is perhaps writing this passage in his later years, when doubters have come to question the eyewitness accounts of the apostles. He wants to assure his readers that their faith is based on the truth. As you read it, picture an old man dictating these words to a scribe. He is wrinkled and bent by the years, but his eyes are young and sparkle with love and joy. He can still picture the scenes of the Gospel as if they were yesterday. Picture those scenes yourself as you read this passage.

1 JOHN 1:1–4

> *What was from the beginning,*
>   *what we have heard,*
>   *what we have seen with our eyes,*
>   *what we looked upon*
>   *and touched with our hands*
>   *concerns the Word of life —*
> *for the life was made visible;*
>   *we have seen it and testify to it*
>   *and proclaim to you the eternal life*
>   *that was with the Father and was made visible to us —*
> *what we have seen and heard*
>   *we proclaim now to you,*
>   *so that you too may have fellowship with us;*
>   *for our fellowship is with the Father*
>   *and with his Son, Jesus Christ.*
> *We are writing this so that our joy may be complete.*

Meditatio: The "beloved disciple" savors the fellowship he has with the Father and the Son. He wants every Christian, and indeed every person, to experience this same fellowship. How has God's word of life been made visible to you on your *Oriens* pilgrimage? Have you seen God's love, felt his presence, or experienced answers to prayer? You too can join Saint John in witnessing that Jesus is alive. Read the passage again, trying to make these words your own words.

Oratio: "I will be with you always, even to the end of the age," Jesus had promised Saint John. And Jesus is with you too. What thoughts, feelings, or desires arise in your heart? Can you put them into words? Speak your words to the Word of life.

Contemplatio: How does Jesus receive what is in your heart? What is in his heart for you? Read the passage a third time, and this time just bask in the fellowship you have with the Father and with his Son, Jesus Christ. Let gratitude rise in your heart, followed by a deep joy. Allow that joy to fill you for a few minutes before moving on.

SUGGESTIONS FOR JOURNALING

1. I have heard, seen, and touched the word of God for myself when …
2. I have experienced fellowship with God when …
3. I sometimes find myself doubting that …
4. I was encouraged by …
5. I ended prayer wanting …

After you've journaled, close with a brief conversation with God giving thanks for your prayer experience. Then pray an Our Father.

December 28 — Tuesday
Fourth Day in the Octave of Christmas
The Holy Innocents, Martyrs

Preparation: *Come, Holy Spirit, enlighten the eyes of my heart.* Be present to the God who is always present to you. Call to mind his loving care for you and spend the first minute of your prayer just resting in the free, unearned gift of loving and being loved. Let gratitude rise in your heart.

Set the Scene: Ask God for a deeper sense of peace and joy in the birth of Jesus, that his light will shine in the dark corners of your heart and your world. Inspired by a star, magi from the East arrive in Jerusalem looking for a newborn king of the Jews. King Herod appeared to welcome them, but secretly was plotting to kill any rival to his throne. When the magi failed to return, he resorted to brutal methods to extinguish the threat. He ordered the massacre of the young boys of Bethlehem. The Christian tradition celebrates these innocent victims as martyrs who bore witness to the Christ Child and were saved by him. Sadly, the Christmas story is not all peace and love. From the very beginning of Jesus' life, darkness sought to devour the light.

MATTHEW 2:13-18

When they had departed, behold, the angel of the Lord appeared to Joseph in a dream and said, "Rise, take the child and his mother, flee to Egypt, and stay there until I tell you. Herod is going to search for the child to destroy him." Joseph rose and took the child and his mother by night and departed for Egypt. He stayed there until the death of Herod, that what the Lord had said through the prophet might be fulfilled, "Out of Egypt I called my son." When Herod realized that he had been deceived by the magi, he became furious. He ordered the massacre of all the boys in Bethlehem and its vicinity two years old and under, in accordance with the time he had ascertained from the magi. Then was fulfilled what had been said through Jeremiah the prophet:

"A voice was heard in Ramah,
　　sobbing and loud lamentation;
Rachel weeping for her children,
　　and she would not be consoled,
　　since they were no more."

Action! Read the passage a second time and play the scene forward. How is God's loving care present in this picture of unimaginable suffering? Picture the Christ Child leading these innocent children into his kingdom. Picture their grieving relatives reunited one day with the children who once were lost, but now are found.

Acknowledge: Read the passage a third time. What thoughts, feelings, and desires rise in your heart?

Relate: Speak to God what is in your heart. Share the burden with him. Look at him and let him look at you.

Receive: What does God want to say to you, or how does he lift your burden? Be open to receiving his answers.

Respond: How does God's response change your perspective? Speak to him about that and deepen the relationship that you have built with him.

SUGGESTIONS FOR JOURNALING
1. How is God's light shining in the midst of darkness?
2. What new way of thinking or responding am I being invited to?
3. How have I personally experienced darkness, confusion, or what seemed like unimaginable suffering?

4. How was God's light shining in my darkness?
5. How is God calling me out of darkness like Joseph was called out of darkness?

After you've journaled, close with a brief conversation with God giving thanks for your prayer experience. Then pray an Our Father.

December 29 — Wednesday
Fifth Day in the Octave of Christmas

Saint Thomas Becket

Thomas Becket was born in London in 1118. Though a cleric of the diocese of Canterbury, he became chancellor to King Henry II and took a leading part in a military expedition against the French. When the archbishop died, Thomas was chosen as his replacement. Perhaps Henry wanted "his man" to be chief cleric in England. However, Thomas took his new responsibilities very seriously and began a life of penance and simplicity. He led a protracted defense of the Church's independence from the crown, which resulted in six years of exile. On this day in 1170, knights and a band of armed men slew him in his church. King Henry did public penance for this crime.

Preparation: *Come, Holy Spirit, enlighten the eyes of my heart.* Be present to the God who is always present to you. Call to mind his loving care for you and spend the first minute of your prayer just resting in the free, unearned gift of loving and being loved. Let gratitude rise in your heart.

Set the Scene: Ask God for a deeper sense of peace and joy in the birth of Jesus, that his light will shine in the dark corners of your heart and your world. Read the passage through. The scene is the majestic and most sacred Temple in Jerusalem, a truly massive and impressive building. There were always worshipers passing through on their way to pray, offer sacrifices, and fulfill the dictates of the law. Picture the bustle of the crowded spaces as you set the scene in your mind.

LUKE 2:22–35

When the days were completed for their purification according to the law of Moses, they took him up to Jerusalem to present him to the Lord, just as it is written in the law of the Lord, "Every male that opens the womb shall be consecrated to the Lord," and to offer the sacrifice of "a pair of turtledoves or two young pigeons," in accordance with the dictate in the law of the Lord.

Now there was a man in Jerusalem whose name was Simeon. This man was righteous and devout, awaiting the consolation of Israel, and the holy Spirit was upon him. It had been revealed to him by the holy Spirit that he should not see death before he had seen the Messiah of the Lord. He came in the Spirit into the temple; and when the parents brought in the child Jesus to perform the custom of the law in regard to him, he took him into his arms and blessed God, saying:

"Now, Master, you may let your servant go
    in peace, according to your word,
for my eyes have seen your salvation,
    which you prepared in sight of all the peoples,
a light for revelation to the Gentiles,
    and glory for your people Israel."

The child's father and mother were amazed at what was said about him; and Simeon blessed them and said to Mary his mother, "Behold, this child is destined for the fall and rise of many in Israel, and to be a sign that will be contradicted (and you yourself a sword will pierce) so that the thoughts of many hearts may be revealed."

Action! Read the passage a second time and play the scene forward in your mind. The Holy Family was too poor to afford the sacrificial lamb. To the outside observer, they would have appeared unremarkable. An old man, himself perhaps easy to overlook, draws near to them. Though his eyesight is probably failing, he can see more clearly than anyone else: this little baby is the long-awaited Messiah, the most important visitor the Temple will ever welcome. And welcome him, he does! Picture the sparkle in Simeon's eyes as he catches sight of this "light for the nations." What is going on in the heart of Simeon? How do Mary and Joseph feel about his words? Can you picture God the Father watching this scene? What is in his heart?

Acknowledge: Read the passage a third time. Focus on the part that speaks to you. What thoughts, feelings, and desires are rising in your heart?

Relate: Speak to God what is in your heart.

Receive: Listen to what the Holy Spirit wants to reveal to you in today's prayer. Will Mary let you hold the Christ Child? What does the Spirit want to reveal to you about this child?

Respond: Give thanks to God and bless him in your own words.

SUGGESTIONS FOR JOURNALING

1. I was surprised by ...
2. The passage that most spoke to me was ...
3. What am I waiting for from God? Am I patient or anxious?
4. Do I desire to be filled with the Holy Spirit, as Simeon was?
5. I ended prayer wanting ...

After you've journaled, close by giving thanks to God for your prayer time today, and then end with an Our Father.

December 30 — Thursday
Sixth Day in the Octave of Christmas

Preparation: *Come, Holy Spirit, enlighten the eyes of my heart.* Be present to the God who is always present to you. Call to mind his loving care for you and spend the first minute of your prayer just resting in the free, unearned gift of loving and being loved. Let gratitude rise in your heart.

Set the Scene: Ask God for a deeper sense of peace and joy in the birth of Jesus, that his light will shine in the dark corners of your heart and your world. Before reading this passage, flip back to yesterday's prayer. The scene is the same tremendous Temple and humble family, who are amazed at the words of Simeon. But now a new person approaches, an elderly woman. Together, Simeon and Anna symbolize the longing for God in every human heart, and faithful Israel grown old awaiting its savior. They also remind us of all the elderly who faithfully worship God and trust in his promises. Perhaps picture a faithful elderly woman you know who seems to always be at church. Read the passage through slowly and prayerfully.

LUKE 2:36–40

There was also a prophetess, Anna, the daughter of Phanuel, of the tribe of Asher. She was advanced in years, having lived seven years with her husband after her marriage, and then as a widow until she was eighty-four. She never left the temple, but worshiped night and day with fasting and prayer. And coming forward at that very time, she gave thanks to God and spoke about the child to all who were awaiting the redemption of Jerusalem.

When they had fulfilled all the prescriptions of the law of the Lord, they returned to Galilee, to their own town of Nazareth. The child grew and became strong, filled with wisdom; and the favor of God was upon him.

Action! Read the passage a second time and play the scene forward in your mind. See the joy in Anna's face as she recognizes this child. See that joy repeated every time she tells the story of seeing the infant Christ. What is in her heart? What is in the hearts of her listeners who are awaiting the redemption of Jerusalem?

Acknowledge: Read the passage a third time, or just focus on the part that speaks to you. What thoughts, feelings, and desires are rising in your heart? What are you awaiting?

Relate: Speak to God what is in your heart. Picture God receiving you with the same joy with which Simeon and Anna received the Christ Child. How does God respond to your words?

Receive: Listen to what the Holy Spirit wants to reveal to you in today's prayer. Receive God's loving care for you like you would hold a precious child.

Respond: Give thanks to God and bless him in your own words.

SUGGESTIONS FOR JOURNALING
1. Today I noticed …
2. I found myself wanting …
3. The strongest image or experience of God's love was …
4. I ended prayer wanting …
5. Anna shared the Good News with others. Who am I called to share this Good News with?

After you've journaled, close by giving thanks to God for your prayer time today, and then end with an Our Father.

December 31 — Friday
Seventh Day in the Octave of Christmas

REVIEW

We will take a break from our prayer time in order to review your *Oriens* pilgrimage so far. As today is the last day of the year, you might also look back on the previous year. If you made an *Oriens* pilgrimage last year, you could pull out your book and flip through it and remind yourself how God was with you last year. Don't make a huge deal out of it, but spend time letting yourself soak in the ways God has walked with you, cared for you, and answered your prayers.

Preparation: *Come, Holy Spirit, enlighten the eyes of my heart.* Call to mind God's loving care for you and spend the first minute of your prayer just resting in the free, unearned gift of loving and being loved. Let gratitude rise in your heart.

Glance through the past week, starting with Christmas Day. What grace and blessings have you received during the Christmas Octave? Here are some questions to help you:

1. Where did I notice God, and what was he doing or saying?
2. How did I respond to what God was doing?
3. I felt God's love most strongly when …
4. I found myself struggling with …
5. I'm grateful for …
6. Have I experienced Christmas more as a season than as a single day? How has this changed my life in any particular, concrete way?

Now go back to your journal entries from the First Sunday of Advent and the first couple of days of the journey.

7. What did I desire as I began this journey? Have those desires grown or changed in some way?

8. Do I notice a particular theme that has been emerging on my *Oriens* pilgrimage?

9. Do I have recurring fears or struggles that Jesus is wanting to address with me?

10. What fruits do I see in my life as a result of my *Oriens* pilgrimage?

11. My strongest sense, image, moment, or experience of God's loving presence so far has been …

_____

_____

_____

_____

_____

_____

_____

_____

_____

_____

_____

_____

_____

_____

_____

_____

_____

_____

_____

_____

Conclude by conversing with God about your week. **Acknowledge** what you have been experiencing. **Relate** it to him. **Receive** what he wants to give you. **Respond** to him. Then savor that image of God's loving presence and rest there for a minute or two. Close with an Our Father.

January 1 — Saturday
Eighth Day in the Octave of Christmas

The Blessed Virgin Mary, the Mother of God

Preparation: *Come, Holy Spirit, enlighten the eyes of my heart.* Be present to the God who is always present to you. Call to mind his loving care for you and spend the first minute of your prayer just resting in the free, unearned gift of loving and being loved. Let gratitude rise in your heart.

Lectio: Ask God for a deeper sense of peace and joy in the birth of Jesus, that his light will shine in the dark corners of your heart and your world. Read through the passage slowly and prayerfully.

NUMBERS 6:22–27

> The LORD said to Moses: Speak to Aaron and his sons and tell them: This is how you shall bless the Israelites. Say to them:
>
> > The LORD bless you and keep you!
> > The LORD let his face shine upon you, and be gracious
> > to you!
> > The LORD look upon you kindly and give you peace!
>
> So shall they invoke my name upon the Israelites, and I will bless them.

Meditatio: Aaron, Moses' older brother, became the high priest at the time of the Exodus from Egypt. This ministry was continued by his sons. They are able to bless the people in God's name. Perhaps use the fruits of your meditation on Simeon to give life to the "shining face" and "kindly look" with which God desires to look upon his people. Read the passage a second time and unpack what these words mean to you.

Oratio: Where do you desire to experience God's blessing in this new year? How has God blessed you in this past year? Reflect on this question, then talk to the Lord about it. Thank him for the blessings of the previous year. Speak to him about the desires in your heart for the coming year. Picture him looking upon you kindly as you speak to him. Then read the passage a third time.

Contemplatio: This time just receive what God wants to give you. What is in his heart for you? How has he blessed you, and will continue to bless you? What does his blessing stir up in your heart? Just receive for a little while before moving on.

SUGGESTIONS FOR JOURNALING:

1. In the past year, I felt most blessed by …
2. The blessing I most desire to receive is …
3. My biggest obstacle to receive God's blessing could be …
4. This new year, I am worried that …
5. I am excited for …

After you've journaled, close with a brief conversation with God giving thanks for your prayer experience. Then pray a Hail Mary.

Week Six

Well Begun is Half Done

I learned a lot about prayer through writing this book. When I made my thirty-day retreat, I was introduced to the words of Saint Ignatius. He told retreatants to begin each prayer time by "Pausing for the space of an Our Father and considering how God our Lord looks upon us." That line never really made sense to me, and it didn't make sense to people I later directed on retreat. I had an epiphany one day when watching an episode of *Tidying Up* with Marie Kondo on Netflix. Before she declutters a house, she pauses to thank the house and the things that it contains. OK, that's a little strange, but I noticed what she was doing. She wants people to begin their decluttering from a place of gratitude, and not from a place of frustration or feeling overwhelmed by all their stuff or fear they will fail at decluttering.

Gratitude! That's what Ignatius was getting at. When we realize what God has done for us, how he has loved us faithfully and sent his Son to die for us, we cannot help but feel grateful. Gratitude is the antidote to anger, the antithesis of a consumer mentality, and the right attitude of a disciple. Our prayer should begin and end with gratitude.

God never stops loving us; the sun will stop shining before God stops loving you. But we don't always feel his love. As I begin prayer today, I might not feel particularly loved, blessed, or cared for by God. But God and I have a history together; I have experienced his loving care in the past, and I am sure to experience it again in the future. So, I begin my prayer by remembering a time that I felt particularly loved, blessed, and cared for. This helps me enter back into that moment and begin my prayer from a place of gratitude.

Saint Ignatius also encourages us to pray a "colloquy," which is a final conversation at the end of our prayer. This is a second opportunity for gratitude. Every prayer should begin and end with gratitude. Mother Church has the same idea when we traditionally pray both a grace before meals and a grace after meals. Our meals, however meager they may be, begin and end with gratitude.

The Church's Morning Prayer is called "Morning Praises" (*laudes*) to begin our day with gratitude. Prayer time at the end of the day is a chance to ask God for mercy (which is why we pray the Act of Contrition before bedtime) and then end the day with gratitude. The word Eucharist means "thanksgiving," as we begin and end our week with gratitude. We should end 2021 with a grateful heart and begin the new year with thanksgiving. Always begin and end prayer with gratitude.

Congratulations on sticking with this book so far! You just passed the halfway point. Know that God has so much more he wants to give you. Don't believe me? Keep walking and find out.

Grace of the Week: This week we get to celebrate the Epiphany twice, once on Sunday and again on January 6. As you recognize the Christ Child as the King of Kings, pray for the grace of a deepening sense of your identity as a beloved child of God.

January 2 — Sunday
The Epiphany of the Lord (Observed)

The word Epiphany means "manifestation." Jesus is manifest as more than just the King of the Jews, but as the king of all the nations. The traditional date of Epiphany is January 6, but in the United States it is celebrated on the Sunday between January 2 and January 8. It is sometimes called "Little Christmas" and marks the arrival of the Wise Men (magi) to the manger in Bethlehem. Saint Matthew saw ancient prophecies being fulfilled by the visit of the magi, who represent the pagan nations. What birthday gift do we have to give to the newborn King of Kings?

Preparation: *Come, Holy Spirit, enlighten the eyes of my heart.* Be present to the God who is always present to you. Call to mind his loving care for you and spend the first minute of your prayer just resting in the free, unearned gift of loving and being loved. Let gratitude rise in your heart.

Set the Scene: Ask God for the grace of a deepening sense of your identity as a beloved child of our heavenly Father. Read through this passage slowly and prayerfully. Spend some time really setting the scene. What is the city like? What do the magi look like? Picture the camels threading their way through the streets of Jerusalem, then Bethlehem. What does the house look like where the mother and child are?

MATTHEW 2:1–12

When Jesus was born in Bethlehem of Judea, in the days of King Herod, behold, magi from the east arrived in Jerusalem, saying, "Where is the newborn king of the Jews? We saw his star at its rising and have come to do him homage." When King Herod heard this, he was greatly troubled, and all Jerusalem with him. Assembling all the chief priests and the scribes of the people, he inquired of them where the Messiah was to be born. They said to him, "In Bethlehem of Judea, for thus it has been written through the prophet:

> *'And you, Bethlehem, land of Judah,*
> *are by no means least among the rulers of Judah;*
> *since from you shall come a ruler,*
> *who is to shepherd my people Israel.'"*

Then Herod called the magi secretly and ascertained from them the time of the star's appearance. He sent them to Bethlehem and said, "Go and search diligently for the child. When you have found him, bring me word, that I too may go and do him homage." After their audience with the king they set out. And behold, the star that they had seen at its rising preceded them, until it came and stopped over the place where the child was. They were overjoyed at seeing the star, and on entering the house they saw the child with Mary his mother. They prostrated themselves and did him homage. Then they opened their treasures and offered him gifts of gold, frankincense, and myrrh. And having been warned in a dream not to return to Herod, they departed for their country by another way.

Action! Read the passage a second time and play the scene forward in your mind. They have made quite the pilgrimage. What was it like? Did they experience frustration? How did they encourage each other? What goes through their minds and hearts as they finally arrive? They find the child with his mother. Picture the relationship between mother and child.

Acknowledge: You, too, have been on a pilgrimage. What thoughts, feelings, and desires are rising in your heart?

Relate: Share your thoughts and feelings with Mary, the Mother of God. How does she respond to you?

Receive: Read the passage a third time. What does the mother want to tell you about her Son? What does she want to tell you about yourself? What is in Mary's heart for you?

Respond: You have a gift to give. Open your treasures and respond by giving the Christ Child your gift.

SUGGESTIONS FOR JOURNALING

1. This time I was most drawn to …
2. I was particularly moved by …
3. The gift I want to give Jesus is …
4. I have been encouraged on this journey by …
5. Who have I encouraged on their pilgrimage of faith?

_____

_____

_____

_____

_____

_____

_____

_____

_____

_____

_____

_____

_____

_____

_____

After you've journaled, close with a brief conversation with God about your prayer experience. Then pray an Our Father.

+

Bless your home today, or plan ahead for a blessing party on January 6. Instructions follow on the next page.

Blessing of the Home and Household on Epiphany

The custom of blessing homes while recalling the visit of the Magi is celebrated in many Old World countries. The family gathers. Candles are lit. It is most appropriate to gather around the Advent wreath in which the purple candles have been replaced with white. But any white, non-scented candles may be lit if the family does not have an Advent wreath.

The leader (usually the father) begins by saying:

Peace be with this house and with all who live here. Blessed be the name of the Lord!

During these days of the Christmas season, we keep this feast of Epiphany, celebrating the manifestation of Christ to the Magi. Today Christ is manifest to us! Today this home is a holy place.

Let us pray:

Father, we give you special thanks on this festival of the Epiphany, for leading the Magi from afar to the home of Christ, who has given light and hope to all peoples.

By the power of the Holy Spirit, may his presence be renewed in our home.

Make our home a place of human wholeness and divine holiness:
a place of joy and laughter, a place of forgiveness and peace,
a place of prayer, service and discipleship.

The leader takes the blessed chalk and marks the lintel (the doorframe above the door) on the inside of the main entrance to the house as follows:

20 + C + M + B + 22
(insert the last two digits of the current year)

The prayer below is said during the marking by another family member, such as the mother or a child:

> Loving God, as we mark this lintel, send the angel of mercy to guard our home and repel all powers of darkness. Fill those of us living here with a love for each other, and warm us with the fullness of your presence and love.

After the lintel has been marked, the leader finishes by saying:

> Lord our God, you revealed your only-begotten Son to every nation by the guidance of a star.
>   Bless now this household with health, goodness of heart, gentleness, and the keeping of your law of love.
>   May all who visit this dwelling find here:
>   the tender loving care of Mary, the God-bearer, the prayerful protection of Saint Joseph, the faithful perseverance of the magi, and the humble peace of the Christ Child,
>   the light of the nations, and thus praise you for all eternity in the unity of the Holy Spirit and the Church, now and forever.

All respond: Amen.

All join hands and pray together the Our Father. The leader then invites all to share a sign of peace.

Other doors may be marked by family members, especially children marking the doors of their own bedrooms. If possible, the family may continue the celebration by sharing a special meal together.

January 3 — Monday
Monday after Epiphany

Preparation: *Come, Holy Spirit, enlighten the eyes of my heart.* Be present to the God who is always present to you. Call to mind his loving care for you and spend the first minute of your prayer just resting in the free, unearned gift of loving and being loved. Let gratitude rise in your heart.

Lectio: Ask for the grace of a deepening sense of your identity as a beloved child of God. Our guide will be the beloved disciple, who wrote the Gospel of John and three letters. He reflects deeply on what it means that God has loved us, and how we are then called to love one another. Read the passage slowly.

1 JOHN 3:22—4:6

And receive from him whatever we ask, because we keep his commandments and do what pleases him. And his commandment is this: we should believe in the name of his Son, Jesus Christ, and love one another just as he commanded us. Those who keep his commandments remain in him, and he in them, and the way we know that he remains in us is from the Spirit that he gave us.

Beloved, do not trust every spirit but test the spirits to see whether they belong to God, because many false prophets have gone out into the world. This is how you can know the Spirit of God: every spirit that acknowledges Jesus Christ come in the flesh belongs to God, and every spirit that does not acknowledge Jesus does not belong to God. This is the spirit of the antichrist that, as you heard, is to come, but in fact is already in the world. You belong to God, children, and you have conquered them, for the one who is in you is greater than the one who is in the world. They belong to the world; accordingly, their teaching belongs to the world, and the world listens to them. We belong to God, and anyone who knows God listens to us, while anyone who does not belong to God refuses to hear us. This is how we know the spirit of truth and the spirit of deceit.

Meditatio: The ancients compared meditating to a cow chewing its cud. Prayerfully consider the words that you read. As we have been loved, so we must also love. And God has given us his Holy Spirit to accomplish this task. But there is another spirit active in the world, a spirit that opposes God. We often call this spirit Satan or the enemy. We need to carefully discern whether something is coming from God or coming from the enemy. He warns us that the words from the enemy will always be welcomed by the world. Do not fear, however, because the one who is in you (the Spirit of God) is greater than the world. Remain faithful to this Spirit and you, too, will conquer the world. Is there a word or phrase that particularly speaks to you? Read the passage again.

Oratio: When have you noticed the work of the Holy Spirit, and when have you heard the voice of the enemy accusing, belittling, or tearing you down? Close your ears to the words of the enemy and open your heart to the Spirit of God. What thoughts, feelings, or desires come from the Holy Spirit? What kind of help do you need to "love one another" as God has commanded you? Tell God what is on your heart and ask for help.

Contemplatio: Read the passage again. This time receive from God's Holy Spirit. Spend a little while abiding in God and letting God abide in you.

SUGGESTIONS FOR JOURNALING
1. When have I experienced being a child of God?
2. Who do I know that reflects God's love in the way he or she loves other people?
3. The voice of the enemy often says to me …
4. The Spirit of God has been telling me …
5. I feel God calling me to a new way of thinking, speaking, or acting …

After you've journaled, close with a brief conversation thanking God for your prayer experience. Then pray an Our Father.

January 4 — Tuesday
Tuesday after Epiphany

Preparation: *Come, Holy Spirit, enlighten the eyes of my heart.* Be present to the God who is always present to you. Call to mind his loving care for you and spend the first minute of your prayer just resting in the free, unearned gift of loving and being loved. Let gratitude rise in your heart.

Lectio: Ask for the grace of a deepening sense of your identity as a beloved child of God, and the gift to share that love with others. Today's passage is very short, but very rich. Read it slowly and savor it. Notice what speaks to your heart.

1 JOHN 4:7–10

Beloved, let us love one another, because love is of God; everyone who loves is begotten by God and knows God. Whoever is without love does not know God, for God is love. In this way the love of God was revealed to us: God sent his only Son into the world so that we might have life through him. In this is love: not that we have loved God, but that he loved us and sent his Son as expiation for our sins.

Meditatio: We were made in the image and likeness of God. Since God is love, we too were made to love and be loved. When we love one another, we live up to our nature. Yet even though we have failed to love, God has loved us so much that he sent Jesus to die for our sins and restore us as adopted children of God. When have you failed to live up to this noble calling? How can you draw strength to love from the one who is love itself? Read the passage again.

Oratio: Since God is love, every experience of true love is an experience of God. When have I experienced true love? How has that love shaped me, challenged me, called me, healed me? What desires arise in your heart? What fears or doubts? Bring them all to God; you can be completely honest with him.

Contemplatio: Read the passage a third time. How does God respond to what you have shared? What does he want to give you? Give God permission to love you. Receive God's love and abide in that love for a few minutes before moving on. Savor the time you have with the one who loves you so unconditionally that he sent his Son as expiation for *your* sins.

SUGGESTIONS FOR JOURNALING

1. When have I experienced the unconditional love of God?
2. How did I respond to that love?
3. I feel most fully alive when …
4. I need God to help me …
5. I ended prayer wanting …

After you've journaled, close with a brief conversation thanking God for your prayer experience. Then pray an Our Father.

January 5 — Wednesday
Wednesday after Epiphany

Preparation: *Come, Holy Spirit, enlighten the eyes of my heart.* Be present to the God who is always present to you. Call to mind his loving care for you and spend the first minute of your prayer just resting in the free, unearned gift of loving and being loved. Let gratitude rise in your heart.

Lectio: Ask for the grace of a deepening sense of your identity as a beloved child of God, and the gift to share that love with others. You may have struggled with accepting God's love for you in yesterday's reading. That's a much more normal response than you may realize. The enemy never stops reminding us of our faults and failures. We humans have a tendency to rely on ourselves, which leads us to fall into sin. The more disappointed we are with ourselves, the more we assume that God must be disappointed too. Yet when we actually take time to draw close to God, we realize that he is rich in mercy. God deeply desires to pick us up, hug us, wash the filth away, and welcome us home. He has placed the Spirit within you so that you might accomplish his good and holy will. The Holy Spirit will help you receive the Father's love more deeply in today's prayer time.

1 JOHN 4:11–18

Beloved, if God so loved us, we also must love one another. No one has ever seen God. Yet, if we love one another, God remains in us, and his love is brought to perfection in us.

This is how we know that we remain in him and he in us, that he has given us of his Spirit. Moreover, we have seen and testify that the Father sent his Son as savior of the world. Whoever acknowledges that Jesus is the Son of God, God remains in him and he in God. We have come to know and to believe in the love God has for us.

God is love, and whoever remains in love remains in

God and God in him. In this is love brought to perfection among us, that we have confidence on the day of judgment because as he is, so are we in this world. There is no fear in love, but perfect love drives out fear because fear has to do with punishment, and so one who fears is not yet perfect in love.

Meditatio: God didn't just give us the Spirit to make us feel warm and fuzzy. He gave us the Spirit because he knows that our own efforts will never be enough to respond to his love. The Spirit allows us to love God in return and to love one another as God has loved us. To the degree that we rely on the Spirit, we will find that the commandment of love is not burdensome. On the other hand, if we rely on our own efforts, we will find the commandment of love completely impossible to fulfill. But more than just action, God also wants union. He wants to remain with you and within you. If God's Spirit is in you, you have nothing to fear. Notice what word or phrase speaks to you most strongly. Read the passage again.

Oratio: Notice the thoughts, feelings, and desires that rise in your heart. Do you welcome God's love for you? Do you find yourself doubting? Do you need to ask for help in trying to love a particularly difficult person or situation — or yourself?

Contemplatio: Read the passage a third time. Receive what is in God's heart for you. Welcome his loving care for you and his desire to bring his love to perfection in you. Remain with God, and focus on God remaining in you.

SUGGESTIONS FOR JOURNALING

1. Have I "come to know and believe in the love God has" for me?
2. What is the biggest obstacle to remaining in his love?
3. The Spirit who moved over the waters is blowing in my life, creating in me …
4. I need help to …
5. I ended prayer wanting …

After you've journaled, close with a brief conversation thanking God for your prayer experience. Then pray an Our Father.

January 6 — Thursday
The Epiphany of the Lord (Traditional)

The liturgical feast of the Epiphany is transferred to Sunday, but there's no reason why we can't also celebrate on its proper day. The Eastern churches refer to this day as "Little Christmas" or "Theophany." Many cultures have special traditions associated with this feast, including parades, special foods, and gift-giving.

Preparation: *Come, Holy Spirit, enlighten the eyes of my heart.* Be present to the God who is always present to you. Call to mind his loving care for you and spend the first minute of your prayer just resting in the free, unearned gift of loving and being loved. Let gratitude rise in your heart.

Set the scene: Pray for the grace of a deepening sense of your identity as a beloved child of God. We will take a little break from 1 John to go back and read the first reading from the feast of the Epiphany. I've chosen imaginative prayer for this passage, but you could also use *lectio divina* if you would prefer. Isaiah is writing to a poor nation of exiles in a foreign land. Picture the dark clouds covering the nations (a reminder of the ninth plague in Egypt, Ex 10:21–29). God's light is shining on his holy people, and they reflect that light to all the nations. Read through the passage slowly to set the scene.

ISAIAH 60:1–6

Arise! Shine, for your light has come,
    the glory of the LORD has dawned upon you.
Though darkness covers the earth,
    and thick clouds, the peoples,
Upon you the LORD will dawn,
    and over you his glory will be seen.
Nations shall walk by your light,
    kings by the radiance of your dawning.

Raise your eyes and look about;
 they all gather and come to you —
Your sons from afar,
 your daughters in the arms of their nurses.
Then you shall see and be radiant,
 your heart shall throb and overflow.
For the riches of the sea shall be poured out before you,
 the wealth of nations shall come to you.
Caravans of camels shall cover you,
 dromedaries of Midian and Ephah;
All from Sheba shall come
 bearing gold and frankincense,
 and heralding the praises of the L*ORD*.

Action! Read the passage again and let it unfold in your mind. See the radiant faces of the people with hearts overflowing. The nations are bringing their wealth as an act of thanksgiving, grateful that God's people have taught them his glory, his truth, and his love. What is going on in the hearts of God's chosen people and the nations that are coming to them?

Acknowledge: What thoughts, feelings, and desires are rising in your heart? Do you realize the precious gift you have been given in knowing the one, true God?

Relate: Share your thoughts, feelings, and desires with God. Above all, let gratitude rise in your heart.

Receive: Read the passage a third time. This time just receive what is in God's heart for you. Savor the loving care you have experienced from him on this Christmas pilgrimage.

Respond: You are meant to be a light. Bask in God's light, receive his love for you, and respond to what he wants to give you.

SUGGESTIONS FOR JOURNALING

1. I felt thick clouds and darkness when …
2. It seemed like God's light was shining on me, and my heart overflowed, when …
3. This Christmas, God gave me the gift of …
4. I ended prayer wanting …
5. God is calling me to be more of a light to the world by …

After you've journaled, close with a brief conversation with God giving thanks for your prayer experience. Then pray an Our Father.

Friday after Epiphany

Preparation: *Come, Holy Spirit, enlighten the eyes of my heart.* Be present to the God who is always present to you. Call to mind his loving care for you and spend the first minute of your prayer just resting in the free, unearned gift of loving and being loved. Let gratitude rise in your heart.

Lectio: Ask for the grace of a deepening sense of your identity as a beloved child of God, and to share the light of God's love with others. There is one more nativity story we haven't read yet. The Bible began, "In the beginning," and then God said, "Let there be light." When Saint John writes about the coming of Jesus, he picks up these same themes all over again. It is a like a new Genesis. Before you begin, flip back and review your prayer time for Monday of the First Week of Advent. Prepare to see the birth of Jesus in a whole new light. Then read this passage slowly.

JOHN 1:1–14

> In the beginning was the Word,
> 　　and the Word was with God,
> 　　and the Word was God.
> He was in the beginning with God.
> All things came to be through him,
> 　　and without him nothing came to be.
> What came to be through him was life,
> 　　and this life was the light of the human race;
> the light shines in the darkness,
> 　　and the darkness has not overcome it.

> A man named John was sent from God. He came for testimony, to testify to the light, so that all might believe through him. He was not the light, but came to testify to the light. The true light, which enlightens everyone, was

coming into the world.

> *He was in the world,*
>> *and the world came to be through him,*
>> *but the world did not know him.*
> *He came to what was his own,*
>> *but his own people did not accept him.*

But to those who did accept him he gave power to become children of God, to those who believe in his name, who were born not by natural generation nor by human choice nor by a man's decision but of God.

> *And the Word became flesh*
>> *and made his dwelling among us,*
>> *and we saw his glory,*
>> *the glory as of the Father's only Son,*
>> *full of grace and truth.*

Meditatio: All the darkness in the universe cannot stop a single point of light. In fact, the darkness is powerless to resist the light. Despite the depth of darkness in our world, God's light keeps shining. So, God's love and God's life are also unstoppable. Have you become a child of God? Have you experienced the Word dwelling among us? Turn over these ideas in your mind, then read the passage again.

Oratio: All things were made through him, and that includes you yourself. Open your heart to the Word of God. Enter into a communion of mind and heart with the Word. Share what is in your heart.

Contemplatio: Jesus lives, as it were, in his Father's heart. And he wants us there with him. Spend a little while abiding in God and letting God abide in you.

SUGGESTIONS FOR JOURNALING

1. When have I experienced being a child of God?

2. How has God's light been shining in my darkness?
3. When have I rejected God's word, God's light, God's life? Why did I choose to reject him?
4. How am I called to be a light shining in the darkness?

After you've journaled, close with a brief conversation with God giving thanks for your prayer experience. Then pray an Our Father.

January 8 — Saturday
Saturday after Epiphany

REVIEW

Preparation: *Come, Holy Spirit, enlighten the eyes of my heart.* Call to mind God's loving care for you this past week and spend the first minute of your prayer just resting in the free, unearned gift of loving and being loved. Let gratitude rise in your heart.

Flip back through your past week's journal entries. As you do, notice what emerged in the conversation. Here are some questions to help you:

1. Where did I notice God, and what was he doing or saying?
2. How did I respond to what God was doing?
3. The darkness feels like …
4. God's light feels like …
5. I found myself struggling with …
6. I'm grateful for …
7. This past week, my strongest sense, image, moment, or experience of God's loving presence was …

_____

_____

_____

_____

_____

_____

_____

_____

_____

_____

_____

_____

_____

_____

_____

Conclude by conversing with God about your week. **Acknowledge** what you have been experiencing. **Relate** it to him. **Receive** what he wants to give you. **Respond** to him. Then savor that image of God's loving presence and rest there for a minute or two. Close with an Our Father.

Week Seven

When Does Christmas Really End?

The liturgical season of Christmas officially ends tomorrow, on the feast of the Baptism of the Lord. But for many people, Christmas has already been over. You probably have a neighbor who threw out their tree on Christmas Day. Christmas music disappears from the radio, and all the Christmas specials are over. Many families try to keep the holiday spirit through the New Year's celebration, but then it's back to work again. Christmas seems to slowly fade into Ordinary Time. When the Baptism of the Lord rolls around, it's more like the Church catching up with the world than a proper celebration of the end of Christmas. Christmas needs a better ending.

It seems that our ancestors found a way to make Christmas last for forty days. In medieval and Tudor England, homes would be decorated with greenery such as laurel, holly, ivy, and rosemary at Christmas time. There was no rush to take it down; it was left decorating the house until Candlemas Eve. Candlemas is the old English name for the feast of the Presentation, celebrated on February 2. This was the day that Jesus was presented in the Temple (see Lk 2:22–40). The Mass for the day welcomes the Christ Child with a blessing of candles and a procession into church.

Even though the liturgical season of Christmas is over, your own personal celebration can continue. I encourage you to keep your Advent wreath and Nativity scene up in the spirit of the old English tradition. Keep praying and keep savoring the light of Christ shining from the manger scene. God has more to give. Let us keep our hearts open to receive.

Grace of the Week: This week we will return to Ordinary Time, both in the liturgical season and also in our lives. Our readings are drawn from the First Book of Samuel. We have seen God present in the shining moments of Christmas. His ordinary presence may be less bright, but keep your eyes open and you will find him no less present. Pray for the grace to see your Savior, Jesus Christ, in a new light, and to hear his voice calling you to follow him.

January 9 — Sunday
Baptism of the Lord

Preparation: *Come, Holy Spirit, enlighten the eyes of my heart.* Be present to the God who is always present to you. Call to mind his loving care for you and spend the first minute of your prayer just resting in the free, unearned gift of loving and being loved. Let gratitude rise in your heart.

Set the Scene: Ask God for the grace to see your Savior in a new light, and to hear his voice calling you to follow him. Read the passage through, slowly and prayerfully. It is the fifteenth year of the reign of Tiberius Caesar and the Spirit of God has called John the Baptist into the desert. He preaches repentance to prepare the people for the Messiah. Read the passage and set the scene in your mind. Picture the wilderness and the great throng of people coming to repentance. Picture their yearning for a savior.

LUKE 3:15–16, 21–22

Now the people were filled with expectation, and all were asking in their hearts whether John might be the Messiah. John answered them all, saying, "I am baptizing you with water, but one mightier than I is coming. I am not worthy to loosen the thongs of his sandals. He will baptize you with the holy Spirit and fire.

After all the people had been baptized and Jesus also had been baptized and was praying, heaven was opened and the holy Spirit descended upon him in bodily form like a dove. And a voice came from heaven, "You are my beloved Son; with you I am well pleased."

Action! Read the passage a second time and play the scene forward in your mind. Jesus, who will baptize with the Spirit, is first baptized in the Spirit. You cannot give what you have not received. What do you want to receive today?

Acknowledge: Put yourself in the scene. What are you longing for or worried about as you hear John proclaiming, "One mightier than I"? Do you desire to be baptized with the Holy Spirit and fire (perhaps a reference to Pentecost)? Are you fearful, doubtful, or eager?

Relate: Jesus himself is praying and has a powerful experience of the Father's love for him. Sit with Jesus by the Jordan River. Share with him what is on your heart.

Receive: How does Jesus respond? Remember, you too were once baptized. What does Jesus want to teach you about your baptism? Be open to whatever God is offering — a word, thought, or feeling, a new understanding or insight? Read the passage a third time and see this moment, and yourself, through Jesus' eyes.

Respond: Continue the conversation for a little while. Then just rest in the love God has for you, the same love that the Father has for his only begotten Son.

SUGGESTIONS FOR JOURNALING
1. I was surprised by ...
2. I was especially moved by ...
3. I sensed God was with me and wanted me to know ...
4. I ended prayer wanting ...
5. I now see my own baptism in a new way ...

After you've journaled, close with a brief conversation giving thanks to God, Father, Son, and Spirit, for your prayer experience. Then pray an Our Father.

January 10 — Monday
Monday of the First Week in Ordinary Time

Preparation: *Come, Holy Spirit, enlighten the eyes of my heart.* Be present to the God who is always present to you. Call to mind his loving care for you and spend the first minute of your prayer just resting in the free, unearned gift of loving and being loved. Let gratitude rise in your heart.

Set the Scene: Ask God for the grace to see your Savior in a new light, and to hear his voice calling you to follow him. Read the passage to set the scene. The ancient world did not understand the complex dance that is fertility. They saw childbearing as a matter of soil and seed (the word semen is the Latin word for "seed"). The man planted his seed in the soil of a woman's womb and everyone waited to see what would grow. When nothing grew, year after year, the woman would have been seen, and considered herself to be, barren soil.

1 SAMUEL 1:1–8

There was a certain man from Ramathaim, a Zuphite from the hill country of Ephraim. His name was Elkanah, the son of Jeroham, son of Elihu, son of Tohu, son of Zuph, an Ephraimite. He had two wives, one named Hannah, the other Peninnah; Peninnah had children, but Hannah had no children. Each year this man went up from his city to worship and offer sacrifice to the LORD of hosts at Shiloh, where the two sons of Eli, Hophni and Phinehas, were ministering as priests of the LORD. When the day came for Elkanah to offer sacrifice, he used to give portions to his wife Peninnah and to all her sons and daughters, but he would give a double portion to Hannah because he loved her, though the LORD had closed her womb. Her rival, to upset her, would torment her constantly, since the LORD had closed her womb. Year after year, when she went up to the house of the LORD, Peninnah would provoke her, and Hannah would weep and refuse to eat. Elkanah, her husband, would say to her: "Hannah, why are you weeping? Why are you not eating? Why are you so miserable? Am I not better for you than ten sons?"

Action! Read the passage a second time and play the scene forward in your mind. Hannah's husband loves her and doesn't hold her infertility against her. But she sees herself as a big failure, and the other wife treats her that way too. Her grief seems to always ruin the family pilgrimage. The narrator blames God for not blessing her with children. What is going on in the hearts of the characters in today's reading?

Acknowledge: Have you felt like a failure? Have you ever felt that God let you down? When have you felt so burdened by grief that you couldn't eat? Notice what is going on in your heart as you read this passage a third time, or just the part that struck you most.

Relate: God is with you. Speak to him about what is going on in your heart.

Receive: How does God respond to the things you are sharing? Hannah is not open to her husband's kindness, but you can be open to whatever God is offering you: a word, thought, a feeling, or a new perspective.

Respond: Continue the conversation for a little while. Then just rest in the love God has for you, the same love that Jesus experienced from his Father at his baptism.

SUGGESTIONS FOR JOURNALING

1. I feel like a failure when …
2. I have been burdened by …
3. I sensed God was with me and wanted me to know …
4. My prayer today gave me a new insight into how I should

think, respond, or act …

After you've journaled, close with a brief conversation with God giving thanks for your prayer experience. Then pray the Our Father.

January 11 — Tuesday
Tuesday of the First Week in Ordinary Time

Preparation: *Come, Holy Spirit, enlighten the eyes of my heart.* Be present to the God who is always present to you. Call to mind his loving care for you and spend the first minute of your prayer just resting in the free, unearned gift of loving and being loved. Let gratitude rise in your heart.

Set the Scene: Ask God for the grace to see your Savior in a new light, and to hear his voice calling you to follow him. Read the passage slowly and prayerfully. Picture the scene in your mind. In the ancient world, people generally prayed out loud to make sure that God heard them. The shrine at Shiloh would not have been a quiet place when it was full of people. Hannah, however, is so emotional that she can't form audible words. This leads the priest to presume that she is a babbling drunk. Could it get any worse for her?

1 SAMUEL 1:9–20

Hannah rose after one such meal at Shiloh, and presented herself before the LORD; at the time Eli the priest was sitting on a chair near the doorpost of the Lord's temple. In her bitterness she prayed to the LORD, weeping freely, and made this vow: "O LORD of hosts, if you look with pity on the hardship of your servant, if you remember me and do not forget me, if you give your handmaid a male child, I will give him to the Lord all the days of his life. No razor shall ever touch his head." As she continued praying before the LORD, Eli watched her mouth, for Hannah was praying silently; though her lips were moving, her voice could not be heard. Eli, thinking she was drunk, said to her, "How long will you make a drunken spectacle of yourself? Sober up from your wine!" "No, my lord!" Han-

nah answered. "I am an unhappy woman. I have had neither wine nor liquor; I was only pouring out my heart to
the Lᴏʀᴅ. Do not think your servant a worthless woman;
my prayer has been prompted by my deep sorrow and
misery." Eli said, "Go in peace, and may the God of Israel
grant you what you have requested." She replied, "Let
your servant find favor in your eyes," and left. She went
to her quarters, ate and drank with her husband, and
no longer appeared downhearted. Early the next morning they worshiped before the Lᴏʀᴅ, and then returned to
their home in Ramah. When they returned Elkanah had
intercourse with his wife Hannah, and the Lᴏʀᴅ remem-
bered her.

She conceived and, at the end of her pregnancy,
bore a son whom she named Samuel. "Because I asked
the Lᴏʀᴅ for him."

Action! Read the passage a second time and play the scene forward in
your mind. The comments of the priest Eli do not discourage her. Hannah has left her grief with the Lord and trusted him to take care of her
problems. Picture her at prayer and again after the little blessing that Eli
gives her.

Acknowledge: What does this passage stir up in your heart — what
thoughts, desires, hopes, fears? Read the passage a third time.

Relate: Take your place on the ground at Shiloh and pour out your heart
to God. Tell him honestly what is burdening you, as Hannah did.

Receive: How does God respond to the things you are sharing? Be open
to receive whatever response you get: a word, thought, or feeling, or just
the confidence that God will take it from here.

Respond: Thank God for whatever he is giving you. Cherish his loving
care for you and rest in it for a few minutes before moving on.

SUGGESTIONS FOR JOURNALING

1. What struck me most was …
2. I felt burdened by …
3. God lifted my burdens when …
4. God answered my prayers with …
5. I left prayer with a new insight, understanding, or confidence that …

After you've journaled, close with a brief conversation giving thanks to God for your prayer experience. Then pray one Our Father.

January 12 — Wednesday
Wednesday of the First Week in Ordinary Time

Preparation: *Come, Holy Spirit, enlighten the eyes of my heart.* Be present to the God who is always present to you. Call to mind his loving care for you and spend the first minute of your prayer just resting in the free, unearned gift of loving and being loved. Let gratitude rise in your heart.

Set the Scene: Ask God for the grace to see your Savior in a new light, and to hear his voice calling you to follow him. Read the passage through. Once Samuel was weaned, Hannah returned to the Temple and presented him to the Lord, as she had promised (see 1 Sm 1:21–28). His family would see him on their yearly visit to the shrine and God blessed Hannah with five more children (2:18–21). Samuel is raised in the Temple and takes care of Eli in his old age. Perhaps Samuel is now sleeping in the very spot where his mother once prayed for the gift of a child. Picture the scene.

1 SAMUEL 3:1–10, 19–20

During the time young Samuel was minister to the Lord under Eli, the word of the Lord was scarce and vision infrequent. One day Eli was asleep in his usual place. His eyes had lately grown so weak that he could not see. The lamp of God was not yet extinguished, and Samuel was sleeping in the temple of the Lord where the ark of God was. The Lord called to Samuel, who answered, "Here I am." He ran to Eli and said, "Here I am. You called me." "I did not call you," Eli answered. "Go back to sleep." So he went back to sleep. Again the Lord called Samuel, who rose and went to Eli. "Here I am," he said. "You called me." But he answered, "I did not call you, my son. Go back to sleep."

Samuel did not yet recognize the Lord, since the word of the LORD had not yet been revealed to him. The Lord called Samuel again, for the third time. Getting up and going to Eli, he said, "Here I am. You called me." Then Eli understood that the LORD was calling the youth. So he said to Samuel, "Go to sleep, and if you are called, reply, 'Speak, LORD, for your servant is listening.'" When Samuel went to sleep in his place, the LORD came and stood there, calling out as before: Samuel, Samuel! Samuel answered, "Speak, for your servant is listening."

Samuel grew up, and the LORD was with him, not permitting any word of his to go unfulfilled. Thus all Israel from Dan to Beer-sheba came to know that Samuel was a trustworthy prophet of the LORD.

Action! Read the passage a second time and play the scene forward in your mind. How many of us would have stayed in bed the third time we thought Eli was calling us? Yet Samuel responds with the same eagerness each time he hears the call. What is going on in his heart?

Acknowledge: Read the passage a third time. Though Samuel was sleeping in the Temple, he never imagined that God himself would speak to him. Do you expect God to call you, or to respond to your prayers? Do you think yourself unworthy of a conversation with the Almighty? What is going on in your heart as you read this passage?

Relate: Share your heart with God, the same God who spoke to Samuel.

Receive: Now it is your turn to listen. Say, "Speak. For your servant is listening." Give God some silent time to respond to you.

Respond: Know that God can call you at any time, and can answer your prayers whenever he chooses. Don't expect God to stop talking just because you have finished your prayer. But for now, be grateful for whatever thought, word, desire, or new insight you might have received in this prayer time.

SUGGESTIONS FOR JOURNALING

1. My favorite part of today's prayer was …
2. I was not expecting …
3. God surprised me with …
4. I can most easily hear God when …
5. What makes it hard for me to listen to God's voice is …

After you've journaled, close with a brief conversation with God giving thanks for your prayer experience. Then pray the Our Father.

January 13 — Thursday
Thursday of the First Week in Ordinary Time

Preparation: *Come, Holy Spirit, enlighten the eyes of my heart.* Be present to the God who is always present to you. Call to mind his loving care for you and spend the first minute of your prayer just resting in the free, unearned gift of loving and being loved. Let gratitude rise in your heart.

Set the Scene: Ask God for the grace to see your Savior in a new light, and to hear his voice calling you to follow him. Read the passage through once. Eli has been a good priest, but he has raised wicked sons. God has prophesied evil against them in response to the evil they have done (see 1 Sm 2:34; 3:11–14). Now we see the prophecies come true.

1 SAMUEL 4:1–11

*At that time, the Philistines gathered for an attack on Israel. Israel went out to engage them in battle and camped at Ebenezer, while the Philistines camped at Aphek. The Philistines then drew up in battle formation against Israel. After a fierce struggle Israel was defeated by the Philistines, who killed about four thousand men on the battlefield. When the troops retired to the camp, the elders of Israel said, "Why has the L*ord* permitted us to be defeated today by the Philistines? Let us fetch the ark of the L*ord* from Shiloh that it may go into battle among us and save us from the grasp of our enemies."*

*So the people sent to Shiloh and brought from there the ark of the L*ord* of hosts, who is enthroned upon the cherubim. The two sons of Eli, Hophni and Phinehas, accompanied the ark of God. When the ark of the L*ord* arrived in the camp, all Israel shouted so loudly that the earth shook. The Philistines, hearing the uproar, asked, "What does this loud shouting in the camp of the Hebrews* *mean?" On learning that the ark of the* LORD *had come into the camp, the Philistines were frightened, crying out, "Gods have come to their camp. Woe to us! This has never happened before. Woe to us! Who can deliver us from the power of these mighty gods? These are the gods who struck the Egyptians with various plagues in the desert. Take courage and act like soldiers, Philistines; otherwise you will become slaves to the Hebrews, as they were your slaves. Fight like soldiers!" The Philistines fought and Israel was defeated; everyone fled to their own tents. It was a disastrous defeat; Israel lost thirty thousand foot soldiers. The ark of God was captured, and Eli's two sons, Hophni and Phinehas, were dead.*

Action! Read the passage a second time and play the scene forward in your mind. The ancient world thought that victory in battle came from their gods prevailing over the gods of their enemies. The people thus believe that the Ark of the Covenant that destroyed the walls of Jericho and brought them safely to the promised land will certainly give them the strength to defeat the Philistines. But the wickedness of the priests is the undoing of the people.

Acknowledge: Where have you felt the sting of defeat? When have you expected God to come to your rescue and, instead of answering your prayers, things got worse? Channel those feelings as you read the passage a third time, or just the part that most spoke to you.

Relate: Now speak to God whatever is in your heart; share your failures and disappointments and defeats with him.

Receive: How does God respond to what you have shared with him? Is there some thought, feeling, or image? Or perhaps a kind of disturbing silence, like he hasn't heard? Sit with it for a little while.

Respond: Continue the conversation, or perhaps answer silence with silence, before moving on.

SUGGESTIONS FOR JOURNALING

1. Where have I felt the sting of failure or defeat?
2. When did God not seem to be answering my prayers?
3. What was one important lesson I learned through failure or defeat or the silence of God?
4. I was surprised by ...
5. A new insight I received was ...

After you've journaled, close with a brief conversation with God giving thanks for your prayer experience. Then pray an Our Father.

January 14 — Friday
Friday of the First Week in Ordinary Time

Preparation: *Come, Holy Spirit, enlighten the eyes of my heart.* Be present to the God who is always present to you. Call to mind his loving care for you and spend the first minute of your prayer just resting in the free, unearned gift of loving and being loved. Let gratitude rise in your heart.

Lectio: Ask God for the grace to see the Lord in a new light, and to hear his voice calling you to follow him. Read the passage through, slowly and prayerfully. Up until this point, there has not been a king in Israel. The twelve tribes have been guided by the judges and the prophets. Sadly, Samuel's sons are no better than Eli's were. And the people want to be like the other nations.

1 SAMUEL 8:4–7, 10–22

Therefore all the elders of Israel assembled and went to Samuel at Ramah and said to him, "Now that you are old, and your sons do not follow your example, appoint a king over us, like all the nations, to rule us."

Samuel was displeased when they said, "Give us a king to rule us." But he prayed to the LORD. The LORD said: Listen to whatever the people say. You are not the one they are rejecting. They are rejecting me as their king.

Samuel delivered the message of the LORD in full to those who were asking him for a king. He told them: "The governance of the king who will rule you will be as follows: He will take your sons and assign them to his chariots and horses, and they will run before his chariot. He will appoint from among them his commanders of thousands and of hundreds. He will make them do his plowing and harvesting and produce his weapons of war and chariotry. He will use your daughters as perfumers, cooks, and bakers. He will take your best fields, vineyards, and olive groves, and give them to his servants. He will tithe your crops and grape harvests to give to his officials and his servants. He will take your male and female slaves, as well as your best oxen and donkeys, and use them to do his work. He will also tithe your flocks. As for you, you will become his slaves. On that day you will cry out because of the king whom you have chosen, but the LORD *will not answer you on that day."*

The people, however, refused to listen to Samuel's warning and said, "No! There must be a king over us. We too must be like all the nations, with a king to rule us, lead us in warfare, and fight our battles." Samuel listened to all the concerns of the people and then repeated them to the LORD. *The* LORD *said: Listen to them! Appoint a king to rule over them. Then Samuel said to the people of Israel, "Return, each one of you, to your own city."*

Meditatio: God is well aware of the corruption that power brings. Instead of serving them, the kings will serve themselves. We often fall into the trap of thinking the right political leader will solve our problems for us. Yet each one seems to be worse than the last. They serve themselves instead of serving their people. Have we been faithful servants of Jesus, our king? Or have we wanted to be like the other nations? Read the passage a second time.

Oratio: The things we struggle with are often problems of our own making. Yet we are quick to point the finger at others. Talk to God about what is on your heart. Then read the passage a third time, or just the part that struck you the most.

Contemplatio: God loves us and doesn't like to see us suffer or be oppressed. Spend a few minutes quietly receiving God's love for you and savoring his presence in your life.

SUGGESTIONS FOR JOURNALING

1. The part that most struck me from today's passage was …
2. I have experienced oppression when …
3. I have been guilty of serving myself when …
4. I reject God's lordship over me in the simple ways that I …
5. I sense God calling me to …

After you've journaled, close with a brief conversation with God giving thanks for your prayer experience. Then pray an Our Father.

January 15 — Saturday
Saturday of the First Week in Ordinary Time

REVIEW

Preparation: *Come, Holy Spirit, enlighten the eyes of my heart.* Call to mind his loving care for you and spend the first minute of your prayer just resting in the free, unearned gift of loving and being loved. Let gratitude rise in your heart.

We have just spent a week with Samuel the prophet. God heard his mother's pleas and gave her a son. She, in turn, gave her son back to God. Samuel was willing to listen to God's voice when others were unwilling or unable. How have you heard God's voice this past week? Here are some questions to help you:

1. Where did I notice God, and what was he doing or saying?
2. How did I respond to what God was doing?
3. I felt God's love most strongly when …
4. I found myself struggling with …
5. I'm grateful for …
6. This past week, my strongest sense, image, moment, or experience of God's loving presence was …

Conclude by conversing with God about your week. **Acknowledge** what you have been experiencing. **Relate** it to him. **Receive** what he wants to give you. **Respond** to him. Then savor that image of God's loving presence and rest there for a minute or two. Close with an Our Father.

Week Eight

He Has Called You Out of Darkness into His Wonderful Light

We will keep walking on the pilgrimage road for two and a half more weeks until we arrive at the feast of the Presentation. You probably know this feast as the Fourth Joyful Mystery of the Rosary. It commemorates the moment when Mary and Joseph brought baby Jesus to the Temple (see Lk 2:22–40).

The law of Moses required the purification of a mother forty days after the birth of a male child (see Lv 12:1–8). It also stipulated that the firstborn belonged to the priests. A firstborn cow, sheep, or goat would be sacrificed to God, but not a child. The firstborn son would instead be ransomed by a payment of money (Ex 13:11–16; Nm 18:13–16). This is a reference to the tenth plague in Egypt, the death of the firstborn, and perhaps the sacrifice of Isaac (Gn 22:2–8).

Saint Luke loves the Temple (his Gospel begins and ends in the Temple, and his symbol is the ox, a sacrificial animal). The way he writes about this moment, Jesus isn't being redeemed but rather *presented*. The unseen God has been worshipped here for centuries. Now God himself, in the person of Jesus, is visiting his own Temple. He comes in the humble form of a little baby. However, his visit does not go unseen. Simeon and Anna are symbols of the whole Old Testament. They have grown old waiting for God's promises to be fulfilled. And they have not been disappointed.

Simeon declares: "My eyes have seen your salvation which you prepared in sight of all the peoples, a light for revelation to the Gentiles, and glory for your people Israel." Remember how back at the beginning of Advent we were told to watch? At this point in history, these two old people are the only ones still watching. And they are rewarded with a vision of the Savior and Lord that all the people are waiting for.

Simeon and Anna perfectly symbolize what our *Oriens* pilgrimage is all about. They recognize Jesus, the light of the world, and they begin to glow with his divine light. May you keep watching for the presence of Jesus and keep reflecting to others his divine light.

Grace of the Week: This week we will use Sunday's reading, the wedding feast at Cana, as our theme. We will delve into the scriptural idea that the love between a husband and wife reflects God's love for his people. Pray for the grace to more deeply appreciate the total gift of Christ the bridegroom to his bride, the Church.

January 16 — Sunday
Second Sunday in Ordinary Time

Preparation: *Come, Holy Spirit, enlighten the eyes of my heart.* Be present to the God who is always present to you. Call to mind his loving care for you and spend the first minute of your prayer just resting in the free, unearned gift of loving and being loved. Let gratitude rise in your heart.

Set the Scene: Ask God for the grace to more deeply appreciate the total gift of Christ the bridegroom to his bride, the Church. Read the passage through and picture the scene in your mind. A Jewish wedding is always a big deal, no matter how poor the couple might be. The feast probably lasted several days. This poor couple didn't have enough wine to go around. Picture a hall full of happy guests. What time of day is it? What time of year is it? What are people wearing?

JOHN 2:1–11

On the third day there was a wedding in Cana in Galilee, and the mother of Jesus was there. Jesus and his disciples were also invited to the wedding. When the wine ran short, the mother of Jesus said to him, "They have no wine." [And] Jesus said to her, "Woman, how does your concern affect me? My hour has not yet come." His mother said to the servers, "Do whatever he tells you." Now there were six stone water jars there for Jewish ceremonial washings, each holding twenty to thirty gallons. Jesus told them, "Fill the jars with water." So they filled them to the brim. Then he told them, "Draw some out now and take it to the headwaiter." So they took it. And when the headwaiter tasted the water that had become wine, without knowing where it came from (although the servers who had drawn the water knew), the headwaiter called the bridegroom and said to him,

"Everyone serves good wine first, and then when people have drunk freely, an inferior one; but you have kept the good wine until now." Jesus did this as the beginning of his signs in Cana in Galilee and so revealed his glory, and his disciples began to believe in him.

Action! Read the passage a second time and play the scene forward in your mind. Notice the panic in the kitchen as the wine runs short, the concern of Our Lady, and the busy servers who begin hauling, by hand, a very large amount of water out of a nearby well. What do Jesus' disciples see and hear and feel? Place yourself in the scene.

Acknowledge: Read the passage a third time. Wine is often used in the Bible as a symbol for joy and gladness. When has the wine run short in your life? What else does this passage stir up in your mind and heart? Are you amazed, skeptical, or just looking to have a good party?

Relate: Turn to Jesus (or Mary) after the scene is over. Have a conversation with one or the other of them, or both. Share your thoughts, feelings, desires, fears. Where is the wine running short in your life?

Receive: How does Jesus (or Mary) respond? What is Jesus telling you to do? Can you see Mary's loving care for you? Be open to whatever God is offering.

Respond: What deeper truth do they want you to realize? After a little conversation, let yourself just enjoy their company for a little while.

SUGGESTIONS FOR JOURNALING
1. The wine ran short in my life when …
2. I felt Jesus (or Mary) saying to me …
3. I need to ask for …
4. The servers put a lot of work into drawing water without grumbling or complaining. Where am I called to work without worrying about the results?
5. When was I surprised by joy?

After you've journaled, close with a brief conversation giving thanks to God for your prayer experience. Then pray an Our Father.

January 17 — Monday
Monday of the Second Week in Ordinary Time

Preparation: *Come, Holy Spirit, enlighten the eyes of my heart.* Be present to the God who is always present to you. Call to mind his loving care for you and spend the first minute of your prayer just resting in the free, unearned gift of loving and being loved. Let gratitude rise in your heart.

Set the Scene: Ask God for the grace to more deeply appreciate the total gift of Christ the bridegroom to his bride, the Church. Inspired by Sunday's passage, we will spend this week on the theme of bridegroom and bride. We begin, once again, *in the beginning.* Read the passage through and picture the scene in your mind. God has created a single man who is living the original "life in paradise." He's perfectly happy naming the animals and living a nice bachelor life. He doesn't know what he is missing until God creates the final masterpiece of creation.

GENESIS 2:18–25

The LORD God said: It is not good for the man to be alone. I will make a helper suited to him. So the LORD God formed out of the ground all the wild animals and all the birds of the air, and he brought them to the man to see what he would call them; whatever the man called each living creature was then its name. The man gave names to all the tame animals, all the birds of the air, and all the wild animals; but none proved to be a helper suited to the man.

So the LORD God cast a deep sleep on the man, and while he was asleep, he took out one of his ribs and closed up its place with flesh. The LORD God then built the rib that he had taken from the man into a woman. When he brought her to the man, the man said:

"This one, at last, is bone of my bones

> *and flesh of my flesh;*
> *This one shall be called 'woman,'*
> *for out of man this one has been taken."*

> *That is why a man leaves his father and mother and*
> *clings to his wife, and the two of them become one body.*
> *The man and his wife were both naked, yet they felt*
> *no shame.*

Action! Read the passage a second time and play the scene forward in your mind. What is Adam thinking and feeling as the scene unfolds? Why does God allow him to live the single life for a while? What does it feel like to wake up and discover the most beautiful of all the creatures, and to realize that she was made for him as he was made for her?

Acknowledge: Read the passage a third time. Notice the thoughts, feelings, and desires that arise in your heart. God knows what you really want and what you were made for. But he wants you to discover it for yourself.

Relate: Turn to God and share with him whatever is on your heart. Tell him what you long for and desire, or how it feels to have a partner who is "bone of my bones, and flesh of my flesh." What more do you still need or want? Speak to your Creator honestly.

Receive: How does God respond to the desires of your heart? What deeper truth does he want to reveal to you? Be open to whatever he is giving you — a thought, word, or recognition of an even deeper desire.

Respond: God is with you. He wants you to be happy. Enjoy the time with the Lord who has been your helper and guide these many pilgrimage days. Savor his company for a few minutes before moving on.

SUGGESTIONS FOR JOURNALING
1. I was perfectly happy when …
2. I need someone to help me …
3. I need to ask for …

4. God wants me to wait patiently so that he can …
5. My deepest desire is …

After you've journaled, close with a conversation giving thanks to God for your prayer experience. Then pray an Our Father.

Tuesday of the Second Week in Ordinary Time

Preparation: *Come, Holy Spirit, enlighten the eyes of my heart.* Be present to the God who is always present to you. Call to mind his loving care for you and spend the first minute of your prayer just resting in the free, unearned gift of loving and being loved. Let gratitude rise in your heart.

Lectio: Ask God for the grace to more deeply appreciate the total gift of Christ the bridegroom to his bride, the Church. The Bible often compares God's covenant with Israel to the marriage covenant between a husband and a wife (see Is 5:1–7; 54:4–8; Jer 2 and following; Ez 16 and 23). In this passage from Saint Paul, we hear that Christ himself is the bridegroom and we, the Church, are his bride. Saint Paul wants us to see Christ on the cross as a man giving himself completely for the one he loves. Bishop David Ricken of Green Bay is fond of repeating, "If you had been the only person on earth, Christ still would have endured all that for you." It might help to have a crucifix present as you pray today. Read this passage slowly and prayerfully.

EPHESIANS 5:25–32

Husbands, love your wives, even as Christ loved the church and handed himself over for her to sanctify her, cleansing her by the bath of water with the word, that he might present to himself the church in splendor, without spot or wrinkle or any such thing, that she might be holy and without blemish. So [also] husbands should love their wives as their own bodies. He who loves his wife loves himself. For no one hates his own flesh but rather nourishes and cherishes it, even as Christ does the church, because we are members of his body.

"For this reason a man shall leave [his] father and [his]

> mother
>> *and be joined to his wife,*
>> *and the two shall become one flesh."*

> *This is a great mystery, but I speak in reference to Christ and the church.*

Meditatio: Turn over in your mind the personal aspect of Jesus' sacrifice on the cross. The Lord of the Universe, who was worshipped by the magi, loves *me*, was born for *me*, and allowed himself to be tortured to death to pay for *my* sins. In his eyes, I am worthy. Jesus nourishes and cherishes *me*. The problem with the Gospel message is not that it's too old-fashioned and boring; the problem with the Gospel message is that it's almost too good to be true. But it is true! Allow the truth of God's personal love for you to sink in. Read the passage a second time.

Oratio: Allow your thoughts, feelings, and desires to rise to the surface. Is it hard for you to accept love? Have you been convinced that Jesus loves everyone but you? Speak to God what is in your heart. Then read the passage a third time.

Contemplatio: Now receive what is in God's heart for you. What does he want to give you — a thought, feeling, or desire? Accept, receive, welcome his love. Give God permission to love you. Then spend a few minutes savoring his love before moving on.

SUGGESTIONS FOR JOURNALING
1. Among the ideas in today's prayer, I find it hardest to accept …
2. I want to believe that …
3. My soul feels at peace when …
4. I felt true love when …
5. I can best respond to God's love by …

After you've journaled, close by offering a few words of thanks to God for his love that you have experienced on your prayer journey. Then pray an Our Father.

January 19 — Wednesday

Wednesday of the Second Week in Ordinary Time

Preparation: *Come, Holy Spirit, enlighten the eyes of my heart.* Be present to the God who is always present to you. Call to mind his loving care for you and spend the first minute of your prayer just resting in the free, unearned gift of loving and being loved. Let gratitude rise in your heart.

Lectio: Ask God for the grace to more deeply appreciate the total gift of Christ the bridegroom to his bride, the Church. In today's passage, the prophet Hosea accuses Israel of being an unfaithful wife, chasing other gods like a married woman chasing other lovers. And yet, despite her unfaithfulness, God remains faithful. Read the passage slowly and prayerfully.

HOSEA 2:14–20

> I will lay waste her vines and fig trees,
>> of which she said, "These are the fees
>> my lovers have given me";
> I will turn them into rank growth
>> and wild animals shall devour them.
> I will punish her for the days of the Baals,
>> for whom she burnt incense,
> When she decked herself out with her rings and her
>> jewelry,
>> and went after her lovers —
>> but me she forgot — oracle of the LORD.
> Therefore, I will allure her now;
>> I will lead her into the wilderness
>> and speak persuasively to her.
> Then I will give her the vineyards she had,
>> and the valley of Achor as a door of hope.

There she will respond as in the days of her youth,
   as on the day when she came up from the land of
      Egypt.

On that day — oracle of the LORD —
You shall call me "My husband,"
   and you shall never again call me "My baal."
I will remove from her mouth the names of the Baals;
   they shall no longer be mentioned by their name.

I will make a covenant for them on that day,
   with the wild animals,
With the birds of the air,
   and with the things that crawl on the ground.
Bow and sword and warfare
   I will destroy from the land,
   and I will give them rest in safety.

Meditatio: God always keeps his promises. He led Israel out of slavery in Egypt, protected them from their enemies, and sent them his Son. How would God feel when his chosen people kept trying out other gods? What about when we stray from right living, have other gods before him, and fall into sin? Let us be ashamed of our unfaithfulness while we marvel at his faithfulness. Read the passage again.

Oratio: God knows your heart even better than you do. Allow your thoughts, feelings, and desires to surface. Listen to your heart, a heart that longs for the love, joy, and peace that only Jesus can bring. What do you need to let go of? What do you need to cling to? Will you choose God as he has chosen you? Ask for the help to do so. Then read the passage a third time, or just the part that speaks to you.

Contemplatio: Sometimes it can be hard to look at God and let him look at you. Recall for a moment his abundant blessings to you at Christmas time. How much he treasures you! Receive what God wants to give you, then rest in his loving care for a few minutes before moving on.

SUGGESTIONS FOR JOURNALING

1. I have experienced the faithfulness of God when …
2. I have felt God's love calling me to …
3. I struggle to believe that …
4. As I end my prayer time, I find myself wanting …

After you've journaled, close with a conversation with God giving thanks for your prayer experience. Then pray an Our Father.

January 20 — Thursday
Thursday of the Second Week in Ordinary Time

Preparation: *Come, Holy Spirit, enlighten the eyes of my heart.* Be present to the God who is always present to you. Call to mind his loving care for you and spend the first minute of your prayer just resting in the free, unearned gift of loving and being loved. Let gratitude rise in your heart.

Lectio: Ask God for the grace to more deeply receive the total gift of Christ the bridegroom to his bride, the Church. We return to the Song of Songs that we meditated on right at the beginning of our *Oriens* journey. Every love story, even Hallmark movies, contain some kind of crisis where it appears the lovers will be lost to each other. This passage captures so beautifully the agony of the lover as she seeks her beloved. Connect, if you can, with the feelings in her heart. Read the passage slowly and prayerfully.

SONG OF SONGS 3:1–4

> *On my bed at night I sought him*
> *whom my soul loves —*
> *I sought him but I did not find him.*
> *"Let me rise then and go about the city,*
> *through the streets and squares;*
> *Let me seek him whom my soul loves."*
> *I sought him but I did not find him.*
> *The watchmen found me,*
> *as they made their rounds in the city:*
> *"Him whom my soul loves — have you seen him?"*
> *Hardly had I left them*
> *when I found him whom my soul loves.*
> *I held him and would not let him go*
> *until I had brought him to my mother's house,*

to the chamber of her who conceived me.

Meditatio: This passage is about more than a lovestruck maiden; it is about everyone who has lost a loved one. We can see in her agony the desperation of everyone who has lost a beloved child, friend, or parent to an untimely death. We can see the searching of Mary Magdalene for the crucified Lord (Jn 20:17). More than anything, two people who love each other long to be together. God loves you and he longs to be with you, as we heard yesterday. But we too long to be with God. Our deepest desire points us to the deep, unconditional love of God. He is the one for whom our hearts yearn and ache. Notice what word or phrase really speaks to you as you read this passage again.

Oratio: Speak to God what is on your heart — your thoughts, feelings, and desires. If you are noticing pain, anguish, or fear surface, don't stuff it back down. Speak to God honestly about it.

Contemplatio: Now receive what God wants to share with you. Is there some new insight or understanding that emerges? Cling to him, hold him fast and do not let him go today. Rest in his love for you for a few minutes before moving on.

SUGGESTIONS FOR JOURNALING

1. I most deeply desire ...
2. Thinking about God's love for me makes me afraid that ...
3. I really want to hear God say or to know in my heart ...
4. I feel most satisfied, joyful, and peaceful when ...
5. I ended prayer wanting ...

_____

_____

_____

_____

_____

_____

_____

_____

_____

_____

_____

_____

_____

_____

_____

_____

_____

_____

_____

_____

After you've journaled, close with a conversation with God giving thanks for your prayer experience. Then pray an Our Father.

✝

The U.S. bishops' "9 Days for Life" novena begins tomorrow. Learn more at www.9daysforlife.com.

January 21 — Friday
Saint Agnes, Virgin and Martyr

Tradition holds that Agnes was a young Roman noblewoman martyred under Emperor Diocletian around AD 304. She is one of seven women mentioned by name in the Roman Canon of the Mass (Eucharistic Prayer I). Her name comes from the Latin word *agnus* meaning lamb. She is often depicted holding a lamb in witness to the innocence of her youth and her virginity. On this day in Rome, the Holy Father blesses the sheep whose wool will be woven into the pallia worn by archbishops.

Preparation: *Come, Holy Spirit, enlighten the eyes of my heart.* Be present to the God who is always present to you. Call to mind his loving care for you and spend the first minute of your prayer just resting in the free, unearned gift of loving and being loved.

Set the Scene: Ask God for the grace to more deeply appreciate the total gift of Christ the bridegroom to his bride, the Church. Read the passage through and picture the scene in your mind. The harlot is the anti-church, as it were, a personification of all the forces of false worship within Israel and in the larger pagan world. She, and all who worship false gods, will be cast into hell. But those who have been faithful to God will be the bride of the Lamb, washed clean in his blood and clothed in righteous deeds. Allow the symbolic language to come alive for you.

REVELATION 19:1–9

After this I heard what sounded like the loud voice of a great multitude in heaven, saying:

"Alleluia!
Salvation, glory, and might belong to our God,
  for true and just are his judgments.
He has condemned the great harlot

who corrupted the earth with her harlotry.
He has avenged on her the blood of his servants."

They said a second time:

"Alleluia! Smoke will rise from her forever and ever."

The twenty-four elders and the four living creatures fell down and worshiped God who sat on the throne, saying, "Amen. Alleluia."
A voice coming from the throne said:

"Praise our God, all you his servants,
[and] you who revere him, small and great."

Then I heard something like the sound of a great multitude or the sound of rushing water or mighty peals of thunder, as they said:

"Alleluia!
The Lord has established his reign,
[our] God, the almighty.
Let us rejoice and be glad
and give him glory.
For the wedding day of the Lamb has come,
his bride has made herself ready.
She was allowed to wear
a bright, clean linen garment."

(The linen represents the righteous deeds of the holy ones.)
Then the angel said to me, "Write this: Blessed are those who have been called to the wedding feast of the Lamb." And he said to me, "These words are true; they come from God."

Action! Read the passage a second time and play the scene forward in your mind. At the time these words were written, the church of Christ was experiencing persecution from Jews and Gentiles alike. Saint John envisions that the Lamb who was slain will win the final victory over his enemies, and his faithful followers will be vindicated. Saint Agnes was a lamb who followed the Lamb faithfully. Where do you see yourself in the scene?

Acknowledge: You have been called to the wedding feast of the Lamb. Have you accepted his invitation and readied yourself for the feast, or are you putting it off as more pressing matters take your attention? Have you allowed other things to take the place of the one true God in your life? Read the passage a third time.

Relate: Turn to Jesus, the Lamb of God. He is humble and patient with you. Share with him what this passage has stirred up in your heart.

Receive: Receive what is in his heart for you. Listen to his words or receive his love, even if it is just a word or a feeling of comfort. Remember that the Lamb is also the Good Shepherd, and you too are a lamb.

Respond: Have a conversation with the Good Shepherd, then relax into his loving care for you for a few minutes before moving on.

SUGGESTIONS FOR JOURNALING
1. The image that really struck me was …
2. I found myself fearful of or disturbed by …
3. The Lamb wants to give me …
4. God is calling me to …
5. In what area of my life do I want to experience his power, his peace, his victory, and his love most powerfully?

After you've journaled, close with thanksgiving to God the Father and to the Lamb for your prayer experience. End with an Our Father.

January 22 — Saturday
Day of Prayer for the Legal Protection of Unborn Children

REVIEW

In the United States of America, today is observed as a particular day of penance for violations to the dignity of the human person committed through acts of abortion, and of prayer for the full restoration of the legal guarantee to the right to life. Offer some fasting or another suitable penance today.

Preparation: *Come, Holy Spirit, enlighten the eyes of my heart.* Call to mind God's loving care for you and spend the first minute of your prayer just resting in the free, unearned gift of loving and being loved.

God always wants to give us more! Flip back through your past week's journal entries. As you do, notice what emerged in the conversation. Here are some questions to help you:

1. Where did I notice God, and what was he doing or saying?
2. How did I respond to what God was doing?
3. I felt God's love most strongly when …
4. I found myself struggling with …
5. I'm grateful for …
6. This past week, my strongest sense, image, moment, or experience of God's loving presence was …
7. How do I feel God calling me to stand against the powers of darkness and witness to the victory of the Lamb?

Conclude by conversing with God about your week. **Acknowledge** what you have been experiencing. **Relate** it to him. **Receive** what he wants to give you. **Respond** to him. Then savor that image of God's loving presence and rest there for a minute or two. Close with an Our Father.

Week Nine

A Sparkler Send-Off for Christmas

A couple of years ago I attended a cousin's wedding. As the reception wore on, I got tired and planned to leave. People were telling me, "The sparkler send-off is coming." I didn't know what they were talking about, and so I left. The next day I saw a printed copy of the schedule. There, in black and white, was clearly listed: Sparkler Send-Off. It was scheduled for just fifteen minutes after I had left. The guests had all lit sparklers, and the couple had walked through them on their way out to their car. When I saw the pictures on Facebook, it made me sorry I had left early. A sparkler send-off gives guests a reason to stick around, if only they knew to wait for it.

In a similar way, the feast of the Presentation is kind of like a sparkler-sendoff for the Christmas season. This final feast day of Christmas is the last time we see Jesus as a baby. Simeon takes the child in his arms and praises God with these words: "*My eyes have seen your salvation, / which you have prepared in the sight of all the peoples, / a light for revelation to the Gentiles*" (Lk 2:30–32). A light! That reminds us of Christmas candles. So, traditionally this feast is celebrated with a blessing and procession of candles, giving it the old English name of Candlemas. We are called, like Simeon and Anna, to go meet the Lord with the light of faith burning in our hearts.

There is just a week and a half left in your *Oriens* journey. How will you continue your prayer once this book has finished? Flip ahead to page 303 and prayerfully consider some of my suggestions for continuing the journey.

Grace of the Week: This week we focus on the call of God and our response. We are called not only to bask in God's light, but also to share it, as Paul and Timothy and Titus did. Ask God for the grace of deeper friendship with him and a deeper "Yes" to his good and holy will.

January 23 — Sunday
Third Sunday in Ordinary Time

Preparation: *Come, Holy Spirit, enlighten the eyes of my heart.* Be present to the God who is always present to you. Call to mind his loving care for you and spend the first minute of your prayer just resting in the free, unearned gift of loving and being loved. Let gratitude rise in your heart.

Set the Scene: We spent Week 7 imagining the early days of Jesus' public ministry. Perhaps you could go back briefly and review the Scriptures from that week. News traveled mostly by word of mouth. By the time Jesus arrives back in Nazareth, people have heard many different reports of his teaching and miracles. Some may be saying, "I knew there was something special about that boy," but others may be wagging their heads and commenting, "He never did anything special when he lived here. What are these reports we are hearing?" Read the passage through once to set the scene. Picture these familiar faces — the local butcher, baker, and candlestick maker — coming to hear what Jesus has to say. Use your imagination to picture the Sabbath morning light shining through the synagogue windows, and the candles and incense wafting through the stone-and-tapestry interior as Jesus stands up to read from the scroll.

LUKE 1:1–4; 4:14–21

Since many have undertaken to compile a narrative of the events that have been fulfilled among us, just as those who were eyewitnesses from the beginning and ministers of the word have handed them down to us, I too have decided, after investigating everything accurately anew, to write it down in an orderly sequence for you, most excellent Theophilus, so that you may realize the certainty of the teachings you have received.

Jesus returned to Galilee in the power of the Spirit, and news of him spread throughout the whole region. He taught in their synagogues and was praised by all.

He came to Nazareth, where he had grown up, and went according to his custom into the synagogue on the sabbath day. He stood up to read and was handed a scroll of the prophet Isaiah. He unrolled the scroll and found the passage where it was written:

"The Spirit of the Lord is upon me,
because he has anointed me
to bring glad tidings to the poor.
He has sent me to proclaim liberty to captives
and recovery of sight to the blind,
to let the oppressed go free,
and to proclaim a year acceptable to the Lord."

Rolling up the scroll, he handed it back to the attendant and sat down, and the eyes of all in the synagogue looked intently at him. He said to them, "Today this scripture passage is fulfilled in your hearing."

Action: Read the passage a second time and play the scene forward with your imagination. The year acceptable to the Lord is a jubilee (see Lv 25:8–13), a whole year that was like a Sabbath. A familiar passage, but with an unexpected twist: Jesus is the fulfillment of these words; in him, the kingdom of God has come. Jesus has long wanted to tell everyone who he is and why he was born. But he has kept silent until now. What is in Jesus' heart as he stands up to read? What is going on in the hearts and minds of his listeners on this Sabbath morning?

Acknowledge: Read the passage a third time. If you have been raised in a Christian household, you have in a sense grown up with Jesus. Perhaps we, like them, have not yet seen the whole Jesus. What is in your heart on this Sunday morning (or whenever you are reading)? What are you thinking, feeling, hoping for, expecting?

Relate: What is the healing you need? Where do you feel poor, or like a captive who needs to be liberated, a blind person who longs to see, or someone oppressed? Speak to God what is on your heart.

Receive: Today, Jesus reads these words to you. Today, this Scripture is fulfilled in *your* hearing. What does Jesus want to tell you or give you right now? Can you open your heart to receive?

Respond: Now respond to Jesus. He will spend all day with you, if you are open to it. Spend a few minutes just resting in the jubilee moment of a God who loves you and has come to meet you.

SUGGESTIONS FOR JOURNALING

1. How did Jesus speak to me today?
2. It can be hard to see my own blind spots. How did my expectations blind me when I began my *Oriens* pilgrimage?
3. God has offered me … (freedom, hope, a new way of seeing, rest, a specific gift)
4. How do I now see Jesus differently?
5. I end prayer with a deeper desire for …

After you've journaled, close with a brief conversation giving thanks to God for your prayer experience. Then pray an Our Father.

January 24 — Monday
Monday of the Third Week in Ordinary Time

Preparation: *Come, Holy Spirit, enlighten the eyes of my heart.* Be present to the God who is always present to you. Call to mind his loving care for you and spend the first minute of your prayer just resting in the free, unearned gift of loving and being loved. Let gratitude rise in your heart.

Lectio: Ask God for the grace of a deeper "Yes" to his plans for your life and to a deeper friendship with him. Today we continue our theme of conversion with the Prophet Jeremiah. When God calls him, he is very aware of his own inadequacy. Yet God assures him that he will give him the strength to accomplish his call.

JEREMIAH 1:4–10

> The word of the LORD came to me:
> Before I formed you in the womb I knew you,
>   before you were born I dedicated you,
>   a prophet to the nations I appointed you.
> "Ah, LORD God!" I said,
>   "I do not know how to speak. I am too young!"
> But the LORD answered me,
> Do not say, "I am too young."
>   To whomever I send you, you shall go;
>   whatever I command you, you shall speak.
> Do not be afraid of them,
>   for I am with you to deliver you — oracle of
>   the LORD.
>
> Then the LORD extended his hand and touched my
> mouth, saying to me,
>
> See, I place my words in your mouth!

> *Today I appoint you*
> *over nations and over kingdoms,*
> *To uproot and to tear down,*
> *to destroy and to demolish,*
> *to build and to plant.*

Meditatio: Who or what has God created you to be? How have you responded to his call? Jeremiah was very aware of his own inadequacy to fulfill the call that God gave him. He will lament about the burden he carries as an unpopular prophet (see Jer 20). And yet he does what God asks. Read the passage again.

Oratio: Speak to him what is on your heart — your thoughts, feelings, and desires. Has he called you to some mission, purpose, undertaking, or lifestyle for which you feel inadequate? Jeremiah does not say "Yes" right away, but is honest with God about his hesitancy. Be honest with God right now; share with him what is on your heart.

Contemplatio: Read the passage a third time. Now just receive what is on God's heart — his response, his assurance, his strength and peace. With God, all things are possible. Spend some time receiving God's love and resting in it.

SUGGESTIONS FOR JOURNALING

1. How has God strengthened me to accomplish a difficult calling or mission, or delivered me from difficulty?
2. I feel called to …
3. But I feel "too young" because …
4. God wanted me to know that …
5. I ended prayer with a deeper sense of …
6. What was I made for?

After you've journaled, close by giving thanks to God for your prayer time today and then end with an Our Father.

The Conversion of Saint Paul, Apostle

How did it happen that Saul of Tarsus, zealous Jewish student of the law and persecutor of Christians, became Paul the apostle who would die for the Jesus he had once blasphemed? He was present when Stephen was martyred and consented to the stoning (see Acts 7:58; 8:1). Perhaps Stephen loved his enemies and prayed for those who persecuted him. Saint Paul went on to become a great missionary of the Gospel in pagan lands. He wrote many of the letters of the New Testament. The site of his burial is now one of the four major basilicas of the city of Rome. Saint Paul reminds us to never despair, for the love of God can conquer even the hardest of hearts. Let us open our hearts to God's love today.

Preparation: *Come, Holy Spirit, enlighten the eyes of my heart.* Be present to the God who is always present to you. Call to mind his loving care for you and spend the first minute of your prayer just resting in the free, unearned gift of loving and being loved.

Set the Scene: Ask God for the grace of a deeper "Yes" to his plans for your life and to a deeper friendship with him. After several missionary trips, Paul returns to Jerusalem against the advice of fellow Christians (see Acts 21:12). He is spotted in the Temple and denounced by some of the Jews as a traitor (21:27–30). A crowd of angry Jews seizes him and drags him out of the Temple shouting, "Away with him!" They would kill him like Stephen if not for the intervention of the Roman soldiers, who pull him from the crowd and carry him to their compound. Paul asks permission to speak to the crowd and then stands on the steps of the compound and speaks to them in Hebrew, their native language.

ACTS 22:3–16

"I am a Jew, born in Tarsus in Cilicia, but brought up in this city. At the feet of Gamaliel I was educated strictly

in our ancestral law and was zealous for God, just as all of you are today. I persecuted this Way to death, binding both men and women and delivering them to prison. Even the high priest and the whole council of elders can testify on my behalf. For from them I even received letters to the brothers and set out for Damascus to bring back to Jerusalem in chains for punishment those there as well.

"On that journey as I drew near to Damascus, about noon a great light from the sky suddenly shone around me. I fell to the ground and heard a voice saying to me, 'Saul, Saul, why are you persecuting me?' I replied, 'Who are you, sir?' And he said to me, 'I am Jesus the Nazorean whom you are persecuting.' My companions saw the light but did not hear the voice of the one who spoke to me. I asked, 'What shall I do, sir?' The Lord answered me, 'Get up and go into Damascus, and there you will be told about everything appointed for you to do.' Since I could see nothing because of the brightness of that light, I was led by hand by my companions and entered Damascus.

"A certain Ananias, a devout observer of the law, and highly spoken of by all the Jews who lived there, came to me and stood there and said, 'Saul, my brother, regain your sight.' And at that very moment I regained my sight and saw him. Then he said, 'The God of our ancestors designated you to know his will, to see the Righteous One, and to hear the sound of his voice; for you will be his witness before all to what you have seen and heard. Now, why delay? Get up and have yourself baptized and your sins washed away, calling upon his name.'"

Action! Read the passage a second time. Paul was as zealous as any Jew for the law of God. After himself persecuting Christians, he had come to believe that Jesus was the fulfillment of the whole law and every prophecy in it. Can you see the love Paul has for those who are persecuting him? Can you feel the presence of the Holy Spirit working in him and through him? What is in the hearts of the mob as they listen to his words? Some of these same people may have shouted, "Crucify him!" Some may have been present when Peter stood up on Pentecost (see Acts 2:14ff), or when Stephen was stoned (Acts 7:51–60). What does this say about God's patience and persistence?

Acknowledge: Read the passage a third time. This time, notice what is going on inside of you. How does Paul's story move you? How have you noticed the Holy Spirit working in your own personal story? How have you cooperated with the Holy Spirit, or fought against him?

Relate: Speak to God what is in your heart. Then turn your attention to focus on God as he gazes at Paul and at the crowd, and at you.

Receive: Let God look at you. Can you see God's patient, persistent love? Receive what is in his heart for you.

Respond: We have come to know and believe in the love God has for us. Respond to God's loving care, then rest in his love for a little while.

SUGGESTIONS FOR JOURNALING
1. If Christianity were outlawed, and I were accused of being a Christian, would there be enough evidence to convict me?
2. If I were to stand up and tell my story of how I came to believe in Jesus, what would I say?
3. I have experienced God's patience when …
4. I have experienced his persistence when …
5. Today God is calling me to …

After you've journaled, close by giving thanks to God for your prayer time today and then end with an Our Father.

January 26 — Wednesday
Saints Timothy and Titus, Bishops

Saint Timothy was the son of a pagan father and a Hebrew-Christian mother, Eunice (see 2 Tm 1:5). He was a disciple of Saint Paul and accompanied him on his journeys. Paul consecrated him bishop of Ephesus. An early legend says he was killed by a mob when he opposed a pagan festival. Saint Titus was also a friend and disciple of Paul, who ordained him bishop of Crete. Paul wrote three pastoral letters to these two disciples. It is fitting that the day after we celebrate Paul's conversion, we celebrate the feasts of two men who Paul mentored in the Christian life.

Preparation: *Come, Holy Spirit, enlighten the eyes of my heart.* Be present to the God who is always present to you. Call to mind his loving care for you and spend the first minute of your prayer just resting in the free, unearned gift of loving and being loved. Let gratitude rise in your heart.

Lectio: Ask God for the grace of deeper friendship with him and a deeper "Yes" to his good and holy will. Read the passage through slowly and prayerfully. Picture Timothy weighed down by the cares of his Christian community in Ephesus, the controversies over false teachings, and the sometimes difficult relationships with the neighboring Jews and pagans. A messenger arrives bearing a letter from Rome. Paul, his old mentor and spiritual father, has sent him comfort and counsel. Imagine the scene as Timothy unrolls the letter and begins to read. What time of day is it? Where is he sitting? What goes on in his heart as he reads these words?

2 TIMOTHY 1:1–8

Paul, an apostle of Christ Jesus by the will of God for the promise of life in Christ Jesus, to Timothy, my dear child:

grace, mercy, and peace from God the Father and Christ Jesus our Lord.

I am grateful to God, whom I worship with a clear conscience as my ancestors did, as I remember you constantly in my prayers, night and day. I yearn to see you again, recalling your tears, so that I may be filled with joy, as I recall your sincere faith that first lived in your grandmother Lois and in your mother Eunice and that I am confident lives also in you.

For this reason, I remind you to stir into flame the gift of God that you have through the imposition of my hands. For God did not give us a spirit of cowardice but rather of power and love and self-control. So do not be ashamed of your testimony to our Lord, nor of me, a prisoner for his sake; but bear your share of hardship for the gospel with the strength that comes from God.

Meditatio: We all need both a Paul and a Timothy. We need someone to mentor us, and we need to mentor someone else in the Faith. Who has been like a Paul to you? Who is your Timothy? Read the passage again. This time remember that all Scripture is inspired by God. The God who loves you guided Paul, through the Holy Spirit, to write these words to you. What is God saying to you?

Oratio: Now speak to God about what speaks to you. Raise your mind and heart to God. Talk to him about the struggles you are experiencing on the road of discipleship.

Contemplatio: Read the passage a third time. Receive what is in God's heart for you, his thoughts and feelings and desires for you, his child. Spend some time resting in God's loving care for you.

SUGGESTIONS FOR JOURNALING
1. The word, phrase, or idea that most spoke to me was …
2. What I really needed today was …
3. God wanted me to know …

4. I ended prayer wanting …
5. Who has been a Paul for me? Who has been a Timothy?

After you've journaled, close with gratitude to God for his loving care for you in today's prayer and all through this *Oriens* pilgrimage. Then pray an Our Father.

Thursday of the Third Week in Ordinary Time

Preparation: *Come, Holy Spirit, enlighten the eyes of my heart.* Be present to the God who is always present to you. Call to mind his loving care for you and spend the first minute of your prayer just resting in the free, unearned gift of loving and being loved. Let gratitude rise in your heart.

Lectio: Ask God for the grace of deeper friendship with him and a deeper "Yes" to his good and holy will. Read the passage through slowly and prayerfully. When you were baptized, you were presented with a lit candle. You were told, "Receive the light of Christ! Walk always as a child of the light. When the Lord comes, may you go out to meet him with all the saints in the heavenly kingdom." You were given the Light of Christ so you could shine with his love and light the way for others.

MARK 4:21–25

He said to them, "Is a lamp brought in to be placed under a bushel basket or under a bed, and not to be placed on a lampstand? For there is nothing hidden except to be made visible; nothing is secret except to come to light. Anyone who has ears to hear ought to hear." He also told them, "Take care what you hear. The measure with which you measure will be measured out to you, and still more will be given to you. To the one who has, more will be given; from the one who has not, even what he has will be taken away."

Meditatio: How is Christ's light shining more brightly now than when you first began your *Oriens* pilgrimage? We who have received must also give generously. Have you been generous to others with the gifts God has given you? Are you a point of light, or do you spread darkness? Read the passage again slowly.

Oratio: Is there a word or phrase that stands out to you? Talk to God about it. Start with thanksgiving for the ways he has enlightened you. How do you feel God calling you to be more a child of the light? How do you feel God calling you to share the light? Read the passage a third time. Then share with God what is on your heart.

Contemplatio: Receive whatever it is God wants to give you — strength for the task, comfort, peace, words of wisdom, silence. Receive whatever he wants to give you, then rest in the warmth of his loving generosity for a few minutes.

SUGGESTIONS FOR JOURNALING:

1. I notice the darkness of the world most strongly ...
2. I saw God's light most clearly in a particular person ...
3. I am a gift, and I am meant to be shared with others. One gift I have to give is ...
4. I shine most brightly when I ...
5. I sense the Lord calling me to a new way of acting, thinking, or living ...

After you've journaled, close with a brief conversation thanking God for your prayer time. Then pray an Our Father.

January 28 — Friday
Saint Thomas Aquinas, Doctor of the Church

Born in 1225 to minor nobility, Thomas's family intended for him to become abbot of the prestigious monastery of Monte Cassino in southern Italy. He was sent to the University of Naples for his theology studies. It was there that he encountered the Dominicans, a new mendicant order that preached the Gospel, lived in poverty, and begged for their food. Against his family's objections, Thomas left the Benedictines to become a Dominican. He is considered one of the greatest philosophers and theologians of all time. The greatest irony was that his classmates, seeing that he was big and quiet, assumed he was quite stupid, and gave him the nickname "The Dumb Ox."

Preparation: *Come, Holy Spirit, enlighten the eyes of my heart.* Be present to the God who is always present to you. Call to mind his loving care for you and spend the first minute of your prayer just resting in the free, unearned gift of loving and being loved. Let gratitude rise in your heart.

Lectio: Ask God for the grace of deeper friendship with him and a deeper "Yes" to his good and holy will. Read the passage through slowly and prayerfully. Try to read it with fresh eyes, an open mind, and a willing heart.

1 CORINTHIANS 12:31—13:13

Strive eagerly for the greatest spiritual gifts.
But I shall show you a still more excellent way.
If I speak in human and angelic tongues but do not have love, I am a resounding gong or a clashing cymbal. And if I have the gift of prophecy and comprehend all mysteries and all knowledge; if I have all faith so as to move mountains but do not have love, I am nothing. If I

*give away everything I own, and if I hand my body over
so that I may boast but do not have love, I gain nothing.*

*Love is patient, love is kind. It is not jealous, [love] is
not pompous, it is not inflated, it is not rude, it does not
seek its own interests, it is not quick-tempered, it does
not brood over injury, it does not rejoice over wrongdo-
ing but rejoices with the truth. It bears all things, be-
lieves all things, hopes all things, endures all things.*

*Love never fails. If there are prophecies, they will be
brought to nothing; if tongues, they will cease; if knowledge, it will be brought to nothing. For we know partially
and we prophesy partially, but when the perfect comes,
the partial will pass away. When I was a child, I used to
talk as a child, think as a child, reason as a child; when I
became a man, I put aside childish things. At present we
see indistinctly, as in a mirror, but then face to face. At
present I know partially; then I shall know fully, as I am
fully known. So faith, hope, love remain, these three; but
the greatest of these is love.*

Meditatio: This passage could be an examination of conscience. We
were made by love and for love. But have we lived up to our calling?
You can put your own name in place of the word "love" and check to
see how you are doing. Ask the Holy Spirit to reveal how you are being
called to love more deeply and authentically. Read the passage again.

Oratio: God is love. As Saint Paul is describing love, he is describing
God. None of us could possibly love like this by our own hard work.
Fortunately, God has given us his very own Holy Spirit. Ask the Holy
Spirit to help you love as you have been loved. Speak to him from your
heart.

Contemplatio: Read the passage a third time. This time receive whatever the Holy Spirit wants to say or give you. Enter more deeply into
communion with the God who loves you. Rest in his loving care for a
few minutes before moving on.

SUGGESTIONS FOR JOURNALING

1. The person who most showed me what true love looks like was ...
2. A recent experience of God's love was ...
3. As I look at the list of what love is, I feel called to ...
4. The Holy Spirit is moving me to ...
5. God has even more to give. I ended prayer yearning for ...

After you've journaled, close with a few words of thanksgiving to God for the gift of his unconditional love as you experienced it today. Then pray an Our Father.

January 29 — Saturday
Saturday of the Third Week in Ordinary Time

REVIEW

Preparation: *Come, Holy Spirit, enlighten the eyes of my heart.* Call to mind God's loving care for you and spend the first minute of your prayer just resting in the free, unearned gift of loving and being loved.

Flip back through your past week's journal entries. As you do, notice what emerged in the conversation. Here are some questions to help you:

1. Where did I notice God, and what was he doing or saying?
2. How did I respond to what God was doing?
3. I felt God's love most strongly when ...
4. I found myself struggling with ...
5. I'm grateful for ...
6. This past week, my strongest sense, image, moment, or experience of God's loving presence was ...
7. I shared God's love when I ...
8. How is God calling me to continue my journey of prayer once *Oriens* has finished?

Conclude by conversing with God about your week. **Acknowledge** what you have been experiencing. **Relate** it to him. **Receive** what he wants to give you. **Respond** to him. Then savor that image of God's loving presence and rest there for a minute or two. Close with an Our Father.

Week Ten

The Journey Continues

Our pilgrimage journey will end in just four more days. Take some time at the end of the road to look back at the beginning of the journey. How has God called you, met you, blessed you? What is he sending you forth to do? As you look back, let gratitude rise in your heart. God always has more to give us, as a priest friend of mine likes to say. Our journey together will be over, but God will continue walking with you in prayer and faith.

One of the things I love about Candlemas is the opportunity to look back to our past and forward to the future. The lit candles remind us of our Advent wreath. As the world grew darker, we lit one candle after another and prepared our hearts for the dawn from on high to break upon us. If you live in the Northern Hemisphere, the days have grown steadily longer and brighter.

The procession with lit candles also reminds us of the blessing and procession of palms that will happen on Palm Sunday. That will be the next time that Mass begins with a procession from the back of church, this time to greet the Lord now fully grown into his role as King and God and Sacrifice.

The lit candles also foreshadow the Easter Vigil, when we celebrate Jesus rising from the darkness of death to shed his peaceful light on humanity. We spent the roughly four weeks of Advent preparing for Christ. Now we have spent forty days celebrating Christmas. In a similar way, one month from Candlemas will begin the forty days of Lenten fasting, followed by fifty days of Easter feasting. The feast of Candlemas calls us back to Christmas and forward to Easter.

Hopefully you too have become a light. Christmas time has lit your heart with the warmth and light of God's love. Keep tending your candle! Keep burning and glowing with the light of faith. Carry that light to the dark corners of the world, that the light of God's love will begin to spread to every heart and home.

Grace of the Week: We will conclude our journey this week with a look at the invitation God offers us to enter his kingdom — and the sobering reality that many can, and will, reject this invitation. Pray for the grace to truly welcome Christ into your heart and to make his love the center of your life.

January 30 — Sunday
Fourth Sunday in Ordinary Time

Preparation: *Come, Holy Spirit, enlighten the eyes of my heart.* Be present to the God who is always present to you. Call to mind his loving care for you and spend the first minute of your prayer just resting in the free, unearned gift of loving and being loved. Let gratitude rise in your heart.

Set the Scene: Ask God for the grace to truly welcome Christ into your heart and to make his love the center of your life. Read the passage through to set the scene. This week immediately follows on last Sunday's passage. I would encourage you to flip back to last Sunday and review your prayer time. We are seated in the synagogue at Nazareth as we hear the passage from Isaiah being fulfilled. But then something goes wrong. Jesus prophesies that they will reject him, and they immediately fulfill his prophecy. It's a terrifying moment of mob rule, perhaps prodded by the same evil spirits that Jesus has been casting out.

LUKE 4:21–30

He said to them, "Today this scripture passage is fulfilled in your hearing." And all spoke highly of him and were amazed at the gracious words that came from his mouth. They also asked, "Isn't this the son of Joseph?" He said to them, "Surely you will quote me this proverb, 'Physician, cure yourself,' and say, 'Do here in your native place the things that we heard were done in Capernaum.'" And he said, "Amen, I say to you, no prophet is accepted in his own native place. Indeed, I tell you, there were many widows in Israel in the days of Elijah when the sky was closed for three and a half years and a severe famine spread over the entire land. It was to none of these that Elijah was sent, but only to a widow in Zarephath in the land of Sidon. Again, there were many lepers in Israel during the time of Elisha the prophet; yet not one of them was cleansed, but only Naaman the Syrian." When the people in the synagogue heard this, they were all filled with fury. They rose up, drove him out of the town, and led him to the brow of the hill on which their town had been built, to hurl him down headlong. But he passed through the midst of them and went away.

Action! Read the passage a second time and play the scene forward with your imagination. Have you ever experienced a moment when someone yelled "Fire!" in a crowded theater, or perhaps seen viral videos of mob attacks? Picture that terrifying moment as you read the scene. This rejection by his hometown foreshadows a future and much darker rejection of Jesus: his crucifixion at the urging of his own Jewish brethren. Somehow the mob loses sight of him for a moment and then he is gone. Notice the emotions in the crowd. Can you place yourself in the scene?

Acknowledge: Read the passage a third time. Notice the thoughts, feelings, and desires that are rising in your heart.

Relate: Are you willing to face rejection for love of Jesus? This is the call of every disciple. Walk quietly through the crowd and join Jesus on his road back to Capernaum. Speak to him of your thoughts and desires, or of your fears and doubts.

Receive: Let Jesus share with you his thoughts and desires. Receive what is in his heart for you, and for the people of Nazareth, and for all who have rejected him.

Respond: Respond to Jesus with gratitude. He is always grateful to find a willing audience. Respond, and then rest for a few minutes in his presence and his gratitude for you.

FOR JOURNALING

1. When have I "risen up in anger," refusing to accept something God was telling me, or a prophet God had sent to

speak uncomfortable words to me?
2. I have rejected Jesus when …
3. I have experienced rejection when …
4. I ended prayer wanting …
5. Where is Jesus in my life right now?

After you've journaled, close with a brief conversation giving thanks to God for your prayer time today. Then pray an Our Father.

January 31 — Monday

Monday of the Fourth Week in Ordinary Time

Preparation: *Come, Holy Spirit, enlighten the eyes of my heart.* Be present to the God who is always present to you. Call to mind his loving care for you and spend the first minute of your prayer just resting in the free, unearned gift of loving and being loved. Let gratitude rise in your heart.

Lectio: Ask God for the grace to truly welcome Christ into your heart and to make his love the center of your life. Picture for a moment a royal wedding. It is outrageous to imagine that anyone would refuse an invitation to such an event. Even more dumbfounding is the realization that many refuse an invitation to a much greater feast: the wedding feast of the Lamb in the kingdom of God. Don't focus on the details so much as on the main point of the parable. Read it slowly and prayerfully.

MATTHEW 22:1–14

Jesus again in reply spoke to them in parables, saying, "The kingdom of heaven may be likened to a king who gave a wedding feast for his son. He dispatched his servants to summon the invited guests to the feast, but they refused to come. A second time he sent other servants, saying, 'Tell those invited: "Behold, I have prepared my banquet, my calves and fattened cattle are killed, and everything is ready; come to the feast."' Some ignored the invitation and went away, one to his farm, another to his business. The rest laid hold of his servants, mistreated them, and killed them. The king was enraged and sent his troops, destroyed those murderers, and burned their city. Then he said to his servants, 'The feast is ready, but those who were invited were not worthy to come. *Go out, therefore, into the main roads and invite to the feast whomever you find.' The servants went out into the streets and gathered all they found, bad and good alike, and the hall was filled with guests. But when the king came in to meet the guests he saw a man there not dressed in a wedding garment. He said to him, 'My friend, how is it that you came in here without a wedding garment?' But he was reduced to silence. Then the king said to his attendants, 'Bind his hands and feet, and cast him into the darkness outside, where there will be wailing and grinding of teeth.' Many are invited, but few are chosen."*

Meditatio: The burning of the city is probably a reference to the burning of Jerusalem by the Romans in AD 70. This led to the destruction of the Temple and eventually to the expulsion of the Jews from Palestine. Christians have interpreted the destruction of the Temple as a result of the rejection of Jesus. The kingdom is now open to all peoples. And yet, as the parable points out, many still refuse to accept the invitation. What invitation(s) has God made to you during your *Oriens* pilgrimage? Read the passage a second time.

Oratio: God does not will the death of the sinner but rather his repentance. God is slow to anger and rich in mercy. God invites us down the road that leads to true life. Rejecting his invitation means to take the path that leads to destruction. Ask God to help you choose the tree of life and reject the tree of the knowledge of good and evil. Share what is on your heart — your thoughts, feelings, desires, hopes, and fears, especially in connection with this invitation.

Contemplatio: Read the passage a third time. Know that God is very close to you; he loves you and he wants what is best for you. Receive his presence and his love. Allow yourself to rest in God's love for you for a little while.

SUGGESTIONS FOR JOURNALING

1. God has invited me to …
2. When I say "Yes" to God's invitation, I experience …
3. When I say "No" to God's invitation, what happens is …
4. I feel moved to ask for …
5. God has promised me …

After you've journaled, close by giving thanks to God for your prayer time today and then end with an Our Father.

February 1 — Tuesday
Tuesday of the Fourth Week in Ordinary Time

Preparation: *Come, Holy Spirit, enlighten the eyes of my heart.* Be present to the God who is always present to you. Call to mind his loving care for you and spend the first minute of your prayer just resting in the free, unearned gift of loving and being loved. Let gratitude rise in your heart.

Set the Scene: Pray for the grace to truly welcome Christ into your heart and to make his love the center of your life. Read through the passage once to set the scene. Think of the ten virgins as bridesmaids, or perhaps torchbearers for the procession of a princely groom. Picture the beautiful wedding ceremony and exquisite feast awaiting the participants.

MATTHEW 25:1-13

"Then the kingdom of heaven will be like ten virgins who took their lamps and went out to meet the bridegroom. Five of them were foolish and five were wise. The foolish ones, when taking their lamps, brought no oil with them, but the wise brought flasks of oil with their lamps. Since the bridegroom was long delayed, they all became drowsy and fell asleep. At midnight, there was a cry, 'Behold, the bridegroom! Come out to meet him!' Then all those virgins got up and trimmed their lamps. The foolish ones said to the wise, 'Give us some of your oil, for our lamps are going out.' But the wise ones replied, 'No, for there may not be enough for us and you. Go instead to the merchants and buy some for yourselves.' While they went off to buy it, the bridegroom came and those who were ready went into the wedding feast with him. Then the door was locked. Afterwards the other virgins came and said, 'Lord, Lord, open the door for us!' But he said in

> *reply, 'Amen, I say to you, I do not know you.' Therefore, stay awake, for you know neither the day nor the hour."*

Action! Read the passage again and let it play out. In ancient times, houses and cities were always locked at night to protect them from bandits, marauders, and wild animals. Still today, most people lock their homes at night for safety.

Acknowledge: Read the passage a third time. Where do you find yourself in the scene? Have you experienced being locked out? What does it feel like?

Relate: God cannot let us into the kingdom if we have not let him into our hearts. Jesus knows the feeling of knocking on the door of a heart only to be told, "Go away; I do not know you." Invite Jesus into your heart today.

Receive: How does Jesus respond to your invitation? What does Jesus bring with him as he enters your heart?

Respond: How does it feel to have Jesus not only with you, but also within you? Jesus lives in the heart of every believer. Let your heart and his heart enter into a deeper communion. Savor the love Jesus has for you for a few minutes before moving on.

SUGGESTIONS FOR JOURNALING
1. I was surprised by …
2. I run out of oil because …
3. The greatest gift God has given me on this pilgrimage is …
4. In response to his gift to me, God is asking me to give him …
5. I ended prayer wanting …

After you've journaled, close with a brief conversation giving thanks to God for your prayer time. Then pray an Our Father.

February 2 — Tuesday
Feast of the Presentation of the Lord

This feast commemorates the presentation of the child Jesus in the Temple forty days after his birth in Bethlehem. Traditionally on this day the priest blesses the church candles that will be used in the coming year. The faithful may also bring candles to be blessed that they will use in their homes. This is the final, formal conclusion of the Nativity of the Lord. The words of Simeon and the procession with candles now point us toward Lent and Easter.

Preparation: *Come, Holy Spirit, enlighten the eyes of my heart.* Be present to the God who is always present to you. Call to mind his loving care for you along your *Oriens* pilgrimage and spend the first minute of your prayer just resting in the free, unearned gift of loving and being loved. Let gratitude rise in your heart.

Lectio: Set the scene by flipping back to your meditations for December 29 and 30. Spend a few minutes back in the Temple with Simeon, Anna, and the Holy Family. A few decades later, this same Temple would witness some of Jesus' strongest preaching. It would also witness the plot of the Pharisees and Sadducees to arrest Jesus at night and to pay the guards to cover up the Resurrection. Pray for the grace to truly welcome Christ into your heart and to make his love the center of your life. Then read today's passage slowly and prayerfully.

MALACHI 3:1-4

> *Now I am sending my messenger —*
> *he will prepare the way before me;*
> *And the lord whom you seek will come suddenly to his*
> *temple;*
> *The messenger of the covenant whom you desire —*
> *see, he is coming! says the LORD of hosts.*

But who can endure the day of his coming?
  Who can stand firm when he appears?
For he will be like a refiner's fire,
  like fullers' lye.
He will sit refining and purifying silver,
  and he will purify the Levites,
Refining them like gold or silver,
    that they may bring offerings to the LORD *in*
      righteousness.
Then the offering of Judah and Jerusalem
  will please the LORD,
    as in ancient days, as in years gone by.

Meditatio: John the Baptist is the messenger sent to prepare the way for Jesus. "Sons of Levi" is a reference to the priests in the old covenant. Is the presence of God something you desire but also fear? How has God been purifying you through your *Oriens* journey? How are you called to offer due sacrifice to the Lord? Read the passage a second time. Notice what word or phrase stands out to you.

Oratio: What have you identified as the deepest desire of your heart? What do you want as this journey ends and a new road begins? Speak to God from your heart. Thank him, tell him your feelings, and ask for the help you need. Then read the passage a third time, or just the part that most speaks to you.

Contemplatio: How does God want to respond to you? What is in his heart for you? Is there a word, phrase, image, or thought that comes to mind? Just receive for a few minutes. God loves you enough to purify you; the perfect offering he desires is the gift of you, yourself. Savor the presence of the God who loves you and is with you in your prayer time today. Just be with him for a few minutes before moving on.

SUGGESTIONS FOR JOURNALING
1. I was surprised by …
2. The part that most spoke to me was …

3. The deepest desire that has emerged in my heart was ...
4. The greatest gift God has given me on this pilgrimage was ...
5. In exchange, I found God wanting me to give him ...
6. I ended prayer wanting ...

After you've journaled, close with a brief conversation giving thanks to God. Then pray an Our Father.

The Presentation of the Lord (Candlemas)

At the Mass:

The people gather in the chapel or other suitable place outside the church where the Mass will be celebrated. They carry unlighted candles. The priest and his ministers wear white vestments. While the candles are being lighted, this canticle may be sung: "The Lord will come with mighty power, and give light to the eyes of all who serve him, alleluia."

Then the priest introduces the Mass:

Dear brothers and sisters, forty days have passed since we celebrated the joyful feast of the Nativity of the Lord. Today is the blessed day when Jesus was presented in the Temple by Mary and Joseph. Outwardly he was fulfilling the Law, but in reality he was coming to meet his believing people. Prompted by the Holy Spirit, Simeon and Anna came to the Temple. Enlightened by the same Spirit, they recognized the Lord and confessed him with exultation. So let us also, gathered together by the Holy Spirit, proceed to the house of God to encounter Christ. There we shall find him and recognize him in the breaking of the bread, until he comes again, revealed in glory.

Then he blesses the candles:

Let us pray. O God, source and origin of all light, who on this day showed to the just man Simeon the Light for revelation to the Gentiles, we humbly ask that, in answer to your people's prayers, you may be pleased to sanctify with your blessing ✠ these candles, which we are eager to carry in praise of your name, so that, treading the path of virtue, we may reach that light which never fails. Through Christ our Lord. Amen.

> Let us go forth in peace.
> The people respond: In the name of Christ. Amen.

Once a Pilgrim, Always a Pilgrim

Pilgrimages always seem to end abruptly. You strive to reach your destination, you struggle on the road, it seems as though you'll never get there. Then you realize it's the final day, the final miles, and the place of pilgrimage is just over the next hill! You have made it to your destination. You bask in the feeling of success, promise to stay in touch with your fellow pilgrims, and struggle to explain to your family what has happened to you.

Then it is back to your old life. But the old life looks different now; the journey has changed you. How did God meet you on the road? What did he teach you? How have you been changed by the journey? What have you been able to let go of that you were carrying for a long time? What have you picked up that you intend to keep carrying?

I always tell pilgrims that they need to keep walking. Our journey is never done until we "come to the end of our pilgrimage and enter the presence of God." Here are some suggestions for you to continue the journey:

- Buy a journal. Start by journaling the questions that I gave you above. At the end of each day, write where you saw God that day. Use the ARRR prayer form to pray with your daily experiences.
- On the following pages, I give you outlines for four different forms of prayer. You might even want to tear out those pages and keep them with your journal.
- Start praying with the daily Scripture readings. You can find each day's readings at usccb.org/bible/readings/ Depending on the reading, you can use *lectio divina* or imaginative prayer (see the Prayer Outlines below) for your prayer each day.
- Subscribe to a monthly missal. I have used Magnificat for years, and I find it very helpful. It includes prayer

for morning and evening, the daily readings, and some reflections and additional prayers. There are many other monthly missals to choose from, and all of them will help you pray daily.

- Need more help journaling? Check out the Monk Manual at monkmanual.com. This resource provides reflection space and prompts for you on a daily, weekly, and monthly basis. It helps you live life with more reflection and purpose.

- Subscribe to my homily podcast. Learn more at PilgrimPriest.us/podcast.

- OSV has a number of Bible study resources. Browse their offerings at www.osvcatholicbookstore.com /product-category/bibles-bible-studies. Consider not only participating in a Bible study, but actually leading one at your local church or in your home.

- Lent is coming up soon. Start reflecting and praying about a theme for Lent and how to live Lent more intentionally.

- Consider making a real, honest-to-goodness walking pilgrimage. My diocese hosts the Walk to Mary every year, a one-day walking pilgrimage. Learn more at walktomary.com. Check out my website (PilgrimPriest .us) for the article "A Step-by-Step Guide to Walking Pilgrimages."

Prayer Outlines

Lectio Divina

Lectio divina can be used with any passage from Scripture. The key is to use Scripture as a conversation starter for a deep, personal conversation with the God who inspired it. Don't rush each step; let them naturally unfold. Remember that the goal is spending quality time with the God who loves you. As you read, think, talk, and listen, you will learn to spend time with God like an old friend.

Preparation: *Come, Holy Spirit, enlighten the eyes of my heart.* Be present to the God who is always present to you. Call to mind his loving care for you and spend the first minute of your prayer just resting in the free, unearned gift of loving and being loved. Let gratitude rise in your heart.

Lectio: Ask God for whatever grace it is you desire to receive in today's prayer time. Read the passage through slowly and prayerfully.

Meditatio: Read the passage again. Turn it over in your mind. The ancients compared meditation to a cow chewing its cud. What was the cultural context? What did the author mean? Perhaps a particular word, phrase, or idea speaks to you. Perhaps it connects to a previous meditation or another Scripture passage. What are your feelings as you read the passage?

Oratio: Prayer must be a conversation between persons. Turn to God and begin a conversation with him. Speak to him what is on your heart — your thoughts, feelings, fears, and desires.

Contemplatio: Read the passage a third time. Now just receive what is on God's heart — his thoughts, feelings, and desires. Spend some time receiving God's love and resting in it. Prayer is experiencing how our Father looks at us with love. Holiness is learning to live in his long, loving gaze every moment of our life.

SUGGESTIONS FOR JOURNALING

Journaling isn't an essential part of the prayer, but I find it helps me to deepen the experience when I put into words what was happening in prayer. You might find questions like these helpful, or you might make your own list of journal questions.

1. The part that most spoke to me was ...
2. What I brought to the Lord was ...
3. God gave me ...
4. I received a new insight, understanding, or sense of myself ...
5. Apply something from the passage to your own life. (For example, a passage about John the Baptist: Who pointed out Jesus to me? When did I point out Jesus to another person, or what virtue of John the Baptist do I feel called to imitate?)

After you've journaled, close with a brief conversation giving thanks to God for the prayer time together. End with an Our Father or another favorite prayer.

Imaginative Prayer

Imaginative prayer helps us disconnect from this present moment in order to connect us with the deep reality of God's loving, invisible presence with us right now. The goal is not to build great imaginary castles in the air. We want to look into the Bible and through it encounter the God who was present in the moment when the biblical passage was written and is present here with you today. The imagination helps to break the ice and start the conversation as you spend quality time with God. It works best with Scriptures that have a lot of visual description or action to them.

Preparation: *Come, Holy Spirit, enlighten the eyes of my heart.* Be present to the God who is always present to you. Call to mind his loving care for you and spend the first minute of your prayer just resting in the free, unearned gift of loving and being loved. Let gratitude rise in your heart.

Set the Scene: Ask God for whatever grace it is you desire to receive in today's prayer time. Read the passage through and picture the scene in your mind. Choose the time of day and the scenery. Populate it with people dressed in period clothes. (Alternatively, you can picture the scene happening in your own city or neighborhood.)

Action! Read the passage a second time and play the scene forward in your mind. Notice how the participants react and what they are thinking and feeling. Notice where Jesus is and what he is doing. (You can also notice Mary, God the Father, the Holy Spirit, etc.) Place yourself in the scene.

Acknowledge: Read the passage a third time. What does this passage stir up in your mind and heart? Pay attention to your thoughts, feelings, and desires. Don't worry if they are "correct," just notice them without any judgment.

Relate: As the scene is finished, spend some time in conversation with Jesus. You can walk with him, sit with him in the scene, or just be aware of his presence in your prayer space. Share your thoughts, feelings, desires, and fears, honestly and openly.

Receive: How does God respond to what you have shared? What is in God's heart for you? Receiving isn't meant to be hard work. It is about relaxing into God's loving presence, focusing on him, and noticing what word, Scripture passage, feeling, or reminder might come.

Respond: This is a chance to deepen the conversation. Ask a question about what God seems to be saying or just say, "Thank you." And like good friends, let yourself just enjoy God's company for a little while.

SUGGESTIONS FOR JOURNALING

1. Something in my life that connected with the story …
2. As the scene played out, what struck me was …
3. I talked to Jesus about …
4. I sensed he wanted me to know, or to give me, or remind me …
5. I left prayer with a new insight, understanding, or a call to a new way of thinking or acting …

After you've journaled, close with a brief conversation giving thanks to God for your prayer experience. Then pray an Our Father or another favorite prayer.

Relational Prayer (ARRR)

Relational prayer is a great way of praying with the experiences of every-day life. No matter what kinds of struggles or challenges you are facing, you can always pause and take a moment to give them to God. Here's how you do it:

Preparation: *Come, Holy Spirit, enlighten the eyes of my heart.* Be present to the God who is always present to you. Call to mind his loving care for you and spend the first minute of your prayer just resting in the free, unearned gift of loving and being loved. Let gratitude rise in your heart.

Acknowledge: Notice what is going on inside of you, your thoughts, feel-ings, and desires. Helpful statements include, "When he did/said/acted that way, it made me feel ____." If you are feeling too angry to concen-trate, pray the name of Jesus a few times and stick with the preparation period until you notice his peaceful presence. With anger in particular, it is helpful to notice what you were thinking and feeling just before you got angry. That can be a clue to where the anger came from, and what God might want you to share with him.

Relate: Share with the Lord what is going on inside of you. Be honest with God. Sometimes we are mad at God himself because he appears to be ruining our lives or ignoring our prayers. You can get mad at God. Tell him how you feel, even if it includes inappropriate words. It's really important that we be completely honest. Do not ask God to give you something or do something at this stage. Just tell him what is going on with you.

Receive: Now we shift our attention from us and our problems to God. This is where I often got stuck when I was learning this prayer form. Picture this scene: I'm struggling with something. A good friend comes and stands next to me. I point out the problem, tell him everything, and he listens patiently. God and I are looking at my problem together. Now, I turn to focus on my friend. What is in his heart for me? How does he look at me? It's his turn to talk. Sometimes it's just knowing that he cares, a feeling of peace, or that I am not alone in my problem. Sometimes it might be a Scripture passage or a few words to put me in my place or add perspective. Like with any good friend, it may not be exactly what I want to hear, but it will be what I need to hear.

Respond: If what he just gave you is hard to receive, tell him so. If it comforts you, thank him. Even if you don't get anything at this time, you can be confident that God will answer you when he is ready and will give you what you really need. So keep your eyes and ears open in case he has more to say or give you later.

Sharing your burdens with God makes them melt like snow in the sunshine. It's almost like magic, but better. We call it grace. Practice this prayer time with the experiences of your everyday life.

Feel free to journal whatever from the above struck you. Then spend a few minutes thanking God for the quality time together, and end with an Our Father or another favorite prayer.

The Saturday Review

I like to keep an old canning jar as a "Gratitude Jar." I start at New Year's and each Saturday I write on a slip of paper the one thing I am most grateful for that week and add it to the jar. At the end of the year, I dump out the jar and review my blessings. If you're interested in adopting this practice for yourself, a Saturday review like those we did throughout the *Oriens* pilgrimage can help fill your jar.

Preparation: *Come, Holy Spirit, enlighten the eyes of my heart.* Call to mind his loving care for you and spend the first minute of your prayer just resting in the free, unearned gift of loving and being loved. Let gratitude rise in your heart.

Flip back through your past week's journal entries. As you do, notice what emerged in the conversation. Here are some questions to help you:

1. Where did I notice God, and what was he doing or saying?
2. How did I respond to what God was doing?
3. I felt God's love most strongly when ...
4. I found myself struggling with ...
5. I'm grateful for ...
6. This past week, my strongest sense, image, moment, or experience of God's loving presence was ...

Journal for a little while whatever you are experiencing.

Conclude by conversing with God about your week. **Acknowledge** what you have been experiencing. **Relate** it to him. **Receive** what he wants to give you. **Respond** to him. Then savor that image of God's loving presence and rest there for a minute or two. Close with a Glory Be.

Acknowledgments

Thank you to Our Lady, Queen of Heaven, who appeared in Champion, Wisconsin, in 1859. Thank you to the Shrine of Our Lady of Good Help for welcoming pilgrims as a place of prayer, peace, and hospitality.

I am grateful to Tim, my first partner on pilgrimage, and all my fellow walking pilgrims through the years. Your companionship has richly blessed and encouraged me.

To Father Paul, Father Tom, Father Michael, and my priestly fraternity group, Father Looney, and the priests and people of the Diocese of Green Bay.

Thank you to the good people of St. John, SS. Mary and Hyacinth, and St. Wenceslaus Parish. Your warm welcome and enthusiastic embrace of *Oriens* helped inspire the 2021 edition.

Thank you to the Institute for Priestly Formation for my training as a spiritual director. This book is a fruit of their ministry, which is why I am donating my royalties to support their work. Learn more at www.priestlyformation.org.

Thank you to my loving family, and especially my parents Jim and Marion, who often tell me they love me and are proud of me.

And to you, my fellow *Oriens* pilgrim. I wrote this book for you. I hope we meet some day, in this life or the next.

The best is yet to come!

About the Author

Fr. Joel Sember was ordained a priest in 2007 for the Diocese of Green Bay, Wisconsin. He has extensive experience as a parish priest and two years of service in campus ministry. He made a thirty-day Ignatian silent retreat and later completed the Spiritual Direction Training Program through the Institute for Priestly Formation in Omaha, Nebraska. He holds a BA in philosophy and Catholic studies from the University of St. Thomas, a bachelor's in sacred theology from the Pontifical Gregorian University, and a license in sacred theology from the Pontifical University Santa Croce in Rome. He has completed a dozen walking pilgrimages. He currently serves as pastor of three parishes in rural northeastern Wisconsin. Between ministry and parish meetings, he rides a motorcycle and paddles a kayak around great Wisconsin lakes. You can listen to his homily podcast every Sunday at PilgrimPriest.us.

About the Artist

Lisa Dorschner is an artist from Wisconsin inspired through prayer, dedication to God, and the ongoing invitation to draw closer to Jesus through faith amidst life's challenges and in gratitude for many blessings. As a full-time art teacher, she encourages her students to seek beauty in the world and share their artwork with others. Lisa is a mother of four, and enjoys being an Extraordinary Minister of Holy Communion, lector, and healing prayer minister for her parish in Oshkosh, Wisconsin.

About the Cover Art

The season of Advent is marked by light overcoming the darkness. Lisa has captured the interplay of light and dark in two different ways. Above, the Christmas star is a light shining in the darkness. Shepherds, wise men, and the Holy Couple can all be seen in silhouette. They are drawn to the light and are moving out of darkness. The eight points recall the eighth day of the Resurrection and the longest point directs us to Baby Jesus. Angels, a camel, and a couple sheep remind us that all creation is groaning in expectation of the Savior. Below, the dawn is just beginning to break over a rugged landscape. One rose-colored hill recalls the third candle of the Advent wreath. The hills show the ups and downs of the spiritual life and encourage pilgrims to keep moving out of darkness and into light, because the "dawn from on high" will soon break upon us.